simply

cupcakes

simply
cupcakes

100 no fuss recipes for everyday cooking

First published in 2012
LOVE FOOD is an imprint of Parragon Books Ltd

Parragon
Chartist House
15-17 Trim Street
Bath BA1 1HA, UK
www.parragon.com

ISBN: 978-1-4454-3763-7

Printed in China

Introduction by Linda Doeser
New recipes by Angela Drake
Additional photography by Clive Streeter
Additional food styling by Angela Drake and Teresa Goldfinch

Notes for the Reader
This book uses imperial, metric, and US cup measurements. Follow
the same units of measurement throughout; do not mix imperial and
metric. All spoon measurements are level: teaspoons are assumed
to be 5 ml, and tablespoons are assumed to be 15 ml. Unless
otherwise stated, milk is assumed to be whole, eggs are large,
individual vegetables, such as potatoes, are medium, and pepper
is freshly ground black pepper.

The times given are an approximate guide only. Preparation times
differ according to the techniques used by different people and
the cooking times may also vary from those given as a result of
the type of oven used. Optional ingredients, variations, or serving
suggestions have not been included in the calculations.

Recipes using raw or very lightly cooked eggs should be avoided
by infants, the elderly, pregnant women, convalescents, and
anyone with a chronic condition. Pregnant and breast-feeding
women are advised to avoid eating peanuts and peanut products.
People with nut allergies should be aware that some of the prepared
ingredients used in the recipes in this book may contain nuts.
Always check the packaging before use.

Picture Acknowledgements:
The publisher would like to thank the following for permission to
reproduce copyright material on the front cover: Cup cakes with pink
icing and sprinkles © Georgina Palmer/Getty Images

Contents

Introduction   6

1   Gorgeous Cupcakes   8

2   Dreamy Chocolate   58

3   Fabulous Fruit & Nut   108

4   Superbly Special   158

Index   208

Introduction

Two, maybe even three, generations have happy childhood memories of birthday party tables spread with all kinds of exciting goodies but almost always featuring a colorful display of frosted cupcakes decorated with sugar sprinkles or candies. However, in the last few years, cupcakes have undergone a revolutionary change. While still beloved by children, they have entered a new era of popularity with adults—and not just as a result of nostalgia. Busy people on their morning rush to the office are now just as likely to buy a cupcake with their latte as a muffin. With all kinds of new recipes, incorporating a wide range of ingredients and flavors, and far more sophisticated decoration than a simple glace icing or buttercream, the cupcake has come of age.

However, they remain just as quick and easy to make at home. Whether made with traditional ingredients and flavorings, such as golden raisins or unsweetened cocoa, or something more unusual, such as cornmeal or saffron, the basic technique is unchanged. It's simply a matter of beating the ingredients together to make a light sponge cake mixture that will rise when baked in a medium–hot oven. Even the most inexperienced cook can whisk up a batch of cupcakes in a matter of minutes. In fact, these days, when most kitchens have electric mixers, making cupcakes is virtually effortless and foolproof. This is one reason why they are such a popular choice for letting children try their hands at helping mom or grandma with baking.

Cupcakes don't have to be decorated, especially if they contain delicious extra flavorings, such as spices, chocolate chips, nuts, or fresh or dried fruit. Risen and golden brown in their neat little paper liners, they are still very tempting. However, decorating them does provide an opportunity to explore your creative side. Simple drizzled frostings and store-bought sugar and chocolate shapes, as well as all kinds of candies, remain popular, but many other ingredients, from preserved ginger to whipped cream and from cream cheese to flower petals, are just as easy. Many of the suggestions in this book are ideal for adults who may not have quite such a sweet tooth as children.

Like all kinds of cooking, but especially baking, when making cupcakes there are some do's and a few don'ts. It is worth reading through the tips on the opposite page to avoid disappointment and to guarantee success.

Top Tips for Success

• Always read through the recipe before you start and check that you have all the ingredients required.

• Do not substitute all-purpose for self-rising flour (or vice versa)—they are not interchangeable. However, if you have run out of self-rising flour, you can use all-purpose flour if you mix baking powder and salt with it—add 1½ teaspoons of baking powder and ½ teaspoon of salt to every 1 cup of all-purpose flour.

• Remove ingredients stored in the refrigerator 30 minutes before using to let them come to room temperature. This is especially important with eggs, which may curdle when added to the mixture if they are very cold. Butter should also be at room temperature, because if it is very soft or even melted, it will ruin the texture of the cakes.

• Measure ingredients carefully—this is more important in baking than in almost any other kind of cooking. Spoon measurements should be leveled off with the blade of a knife. Do not pour small quantities of liquid, such as vanilla extract, into a measuring spoon held over the mixing bowl to avoid overfilling and so ruining the flavor of your cakes. The cup for measuring larger amounts of liquid should stand on a flat surface and you should check the measure at eye level.

• Using an electric mixer is quick and easy, but be careful not to overbeat the mixture. A wooden spoon works just as well but requires a little more time and effort.

• Once you have mixed the cake batter, do not let it stand for any length of time, but spoon it immediately into the paper liners and bake, otherwise your cakes may be disappointingly flat.

• Do not overfill the paper liners or the mixture will bubble over during cooking, creating misshapen cakes and a mess in the oven.

• Always preheat the oven to the specified temperature, otherwise the cakes may not rise evenly or at all.

• Bake the cakes on a shelf toward the top of a conventional oven. If they are too high, the tops may become brown before the insides are cooked through. If they are too low, they will take too long to cook and will dry out. However, the temperature in convection ovens is even throughout

1

Gorgeous
Cupcakes

vanilla frosted cupcakes

MAKES 12

½ **cup butter, softened**

generous ½ **cup superfine sugar**

2 **eggs, lightly beaten**

1 **cup self-rising flour**

1 **tbsp milk**

1 **tbsp colored sprinkles**

frosting

¾ **cup unsalted butter, softened**

1 **tsp vanilla extract**

2½ **cups confectioners' sugar**

1 Preheat the oven to 350°F/180°C. Put 12 paper liners in a muffin pan or put 12 double-layer paper liners on a baking sheet.

2 Put the butter and sugar in a bowl and beat together until light and fluffy. Gradually beat in the eggs. Sift over the flour and, using a metal spoon, fold into the mixture with the milk. Spoon the batter into the paper liners.

3 Bake the cupcakes in the preheated oven for 20 minutes, or until golden brown and firm to the touch. Transfer to a wire rack and let cool.

4 To make the frosting, put the butter and vanilla extract in a bowl and, using an electric mixer, beat until the butter is pale and very soft. Gradually sift in the confectioners' sugar, beating well after each addition. Spoon the frosting into a large pastry bag fitted with a medium star-shaped tip and pipe large swirls of frosting on the top of each cupcake. Sprinkle with colored sprinkles.

fairy cupcakes

MAKES 16

½ cup butter

generous ½ cup superfine sugar

2 eggs, beaten

1 cup self-rising flour

sugar flowers, sprinkles, candied cherries, and/ or chocolate strands, to decorate

icing

1¾ cups confectioners' sugar

about 2 tbsp warm water

a few drops of food coloring (optional)

1 Preheat the oven to 375°F/190°C. Place 16 paper liners into 2 shallow muffin pans or put 16 double-layer paper liners on 2 baking sheets.

2 Place the butter and sugar in a large bowl and cream together with a wooden spoon or electric mixer until pale and fluffy.

3 Gradually add the eggs, beating well after each addition. Fold in the flour lightly and evenly, using a metal spoon. Divide the batter among the paper liners and bake in the preheated oven for 15–20 minutes. Transfer to a wire rack and let cool.

4 For the icing, sift the confectioners' sugar into a bowl and stir in just enough water to mix to a smooth paste that is thick enough to coat the back of a wooden spoon. Stir in a few drops of food coloring, if using, then spread the icing over the cupcakes and decorate as desired.

mini candy cupcakes

MAKES 18

generous ⅓ cup self-rising flour

¼ tsp baking powder

4 tbsp soft margarine

¼ cup superfine sugar

1 egg, lightly beaten

candies, such as gum drops, licorice, and sugar-coated chocolate candies, to decorate

icing

¾ cup confectioners' sugar

2–3 tsp water

1 Preheat the oven to 350°F/180°C. Put 18 paper liners in a muffin pan or put 18 double-layer paper liners on a baking sheet.

2 Sift the flour and baking powder into a bowl. Add the margarine, sugar, and egg and, using an electric mixer, beat together until smooth. Spoon the batter into the paper liners.

3 Bake the cupcakes in the preheated oven for 15–20 minutes, until risen and golden brown. Transfer to a wire rack and let cool.

4 To make the icing, sift the confectioners' sugar into a bowl and beat in the water to make a smooth thick icing. Spoon a little icing in the center of each cupcake and decorate each with a candy. Let set.

rose petal cupcakes

MAKES 12

½ **cup butter, softened**

generous ½ cup superfine sugar

2 eggs, lightly beaten

1 tbsp milk

few drops of extract of rose oil

¼ tsp vanilla extract

scant 1¼ cups self-rising flour

candied rose petals and silver dragées (cake decoration balls), to decorate

frosting

6 tbsp butter, softened

1½ cups confectioners' sugar

pink food coloring (optional)

1 Preheat the oven to 400°F/200°C. Put 12 paper liners in a muffin pan, or put 12 double-layer paper liners on a baking sheet.

2 Put the butter and sugar in a bowl and beat together until light and fluffy. Gradually add the eggs, beating well after each addition. Stir in the milk, rose oil extract, and vanilla extract, then, using a metal spoon, fold in the flour. Spoon the batter into the paper liners. Bake the cupcakes in the preheated oven for 12–15 minutes, until well risen and golden brown. Transfer to a wire rack and let cool.

3 To make the frosting, put the butter in a large bowl and beat until fluffy. Sift in the confectioners' sugar and mix well together. If desired, add a few drops of pink food coloring to complement the rose petals.

4 When the cupcakes are cold, spread the frosting on top of each cake. Top with 1–2 candied rose petals and sprinkle with silver dragées to decorate.

Step 2

Step 3

Step 4

pink & white cupcakes

MAKES 16

generous ¾ cup self-rising flour

1 tsp baking powder

½ cup butter, softened

generous ½ cup superfine sugar

2 eggs, lightly beaten

1 tbsp milk

few drops red food coloring

topping

1 egg white

generous ¾ cup superfine sugar

2 tbsp hot water

large pinch of cream of tartar

2 tbsp raspberry jelly

3 tbsp dry unsweetened flaked coconut, lightly toasted

1 Preheat the oven to 350°F/180°C. Put 16 paper liners in 2 muffin pans or put 16 double-layer paper liners on a large baking sheet.

2 Sift the flour and baking powder into a bowl. Add the butter, sugar, and eggs and, using an electric mixer, beat together until smooth. Mix together the milk and food coloring and stir into the batter until evenly blended. Spoon the batter into the paper liners.

3 Bake the cupcakes in the preheated oven for 20 minutes, or until risen and golden brown. Transfer to a wire rack and let cool.

4 To make the topping, put the egg white, sugar, water, and cream of tartar in a heatproof bowl set over a saucepan of simmering water. Using an electric mixer, beat for 5–6 minutes, until the frosting is thick and makes soft peaks when the mixer is lifted out.

5 Spread a layer of raspberry jelly over each cupcake, and then swirl over the frosting. Sprinkle with the toasted coconut.

lemon cornmeal cupcakes

MAKES 14

½ cup butter, softened

½ cup superfine sugar

finely grated rind and juice of ½ lemon

2 eggs lightly beaten

generous ⅓ cup all-purpose flour

1 tsp baking powder

⅓ cup quick-cooking cornmeal or instant polenta

candied violets, to decorate

frosting

5½ oz/150 g mascarpone cheese

2 tsp finely grated lemon rind

¼ cup confectioners' sugar

1 Preheat the oven to 350°F/180°C. Put 14 paper liners in 2 muffin pans or put 14 double-layer paper liners on a baking sheet.

2 Put the butter and sugar in a bowl and beat together until light and fluffy. Beat in the lemon rind and juice. Gradually beat in the eggs. Sift in the flour and baking powder and, using a metal spoon, fold gently into the mixture with the cornmeal. Spoon the batter into the paper liners.

3 Bake the cupcakes in the preheated oven for 20 minutes, or golden brown and firm to the touch. Transfer to a wire rack and let cool.

4 To make the frosting, beat the mascarpone cheese until smooth, then beat in the lemon rind and confectioners' sugar. Spread the frosting over the cupcakes. Store the cupcakes in the refrigerator until ready to serve. Decorate each cupcake with a candied violet just before serving.

iced almond & lemon cupcakes

MAKES 16

½ cup butter, softened

generous ½ cup superfine sugar

finely grated rind of ½ lemon

2 extra large eggs, lightly beaten

1¼ cups self-rising flour

generous ⅓ cup ground almonds

⅓ cup candied citron peel, thinly sliced

icing

½ cup confectioners' sugar

3 tsp warm water

1 Preheat the oven to 350°F/180°C. Put 16 paper liners in 2 muffin pans or put 16 double-layer paper liners on a baking sheet.

2 Put the butter, sugar, and lemon rind in a bowl and beat together until light and fluffy. Gradually beat in the eggs. Sift in the flour and, using a metal spoon, fold gently into the batter with the ground almonds. Spoon the batter into the paper liners. Put a slice of citron peel on the top of each cupcake.

3 Bake the cupcakes in the preheated oven for 20–25 minutes, or until risen and golden brown. Transfer to a wire rack and let cool.

4 To make the icing, sift the confectioners' sugar into a bowl and add enough of the warm water to make a runny icing. Using a pastry brush, glaze the top of each cupcake with the icing. Let set.

poppy seed & orange cupcakes

MAKES 12

2 tbsp poppy seeds

2 tbsp hot milk

6 tbsp butter, softened

scant ½ cup superfine sugar

finely grated rind of ½ orange

1 extra large egg, lightly beaten

¾ cup self-rising flour

frosting

6 tbsp butter, softened

finely grated rind of ½ orange

1½ cups confectioners' sugar

1–2 tbsp orange juice

1 Preheat the oven to 350°F/180°C. Put 12 paper liners in a muffin pan or put 12 double-layer paper liners on a baking sheet. Place the poppy seeds and milk in a small bowl and set aside for 10 minutes.

2 Put the butter, sugar, and orange rind in a bowl and beat together until light and fluffy. Gradually beat in the egg. Sift in the flour and, using a metal spoon, fold gently into the batter with the poppy seeds and milk. Spoon the batter into the paper liners.

3 Bake the cupcakes in the preheated oven for 20 minutes, or until risen and golden brown. Transfer to a wire rack and let cool.

4 To make the frosting, put the butter and orange rind in a bowl and beat until fluffy. Gradually beat in the confectioners' sugar and enough orange juice to make a smooth and creamy frosting. Swirl the frosting over the top of the cupcakes.

Step 1

Step 2

Step 3

warm strawberry cupcakes

MAKES 6

4 tbsp strawberry jelly

½ cup butter, softened, plus extra for greasing

generous ½ cup superfine sugar

2 eggs, lightly beaten

1 tsp vanilla extract

generous ¾ cup self-rising flour

1 lb/450 g small whole fresh strawberries

confectioners' sugar, for dusting

1 Preheat the oven to 350°F/180°C. Grease six ¾-cup ovenproof dishes (such as ramekins) with butter. Spoon 2 teaspoons of the strawberry jelly in the bottom of each dish.

2 Put the butter and sugar in a bowl and beat together until light and fluffy. Gradually add the eggs, beating well after each addition, then add the vanilla extract. Sift in the flour and, using a large metal spoon, fold it into the mixture. Spoon the batter into the dishes.

3 Stand the dishes in a roasting pan, then pour in enough hot water to come one-third up the sides of the dishes. Bake the cupcakes in the preheated oven for 40 minutes, or until well risen and a skewer inserted in the centre comes out clean. If overbrowning, cover the cupcakes with a sheet of foil. Let the cupcakes cool for 2–3 minutes, then carefully lift the dishes from the pan.

4 Place a few of the whole strawberries on each cake, then dust them with sifted confectioners' sugar. Serve warm with the remaining strawberries.

caramel cupcakes

MAKES 12

6 tbsp butter, softened

¼ cup dark brown sugar

1 tbsp dark corn syrup

1 extra large egg, lightly beaten

¾ cup self-rising flour

1 tsp grated nutmeg

2 tbsp milk

frosting

½ cup light brown sugar

1 medium egg white

1 tbsp hot water

pinch of cream of tartar

1 Preheat the oven to 350°F/180°C. Put 12 paper liners in a muffin pan or put 12 double-layer paper liners on a baking sheet.

2 Put the butter, sugar, and corn syrup in a bowl and beat together until light and fluffy. Gradually beat in the egg. Sift in the flour and, using a metal spoon, fold gently into the batter with the nutmeg and milk. Spoon the batter into the paper liners.

3 Bake the cupcakes in the preheated oven for 15–20 minutes, or until risen and golden brown. Transfer to a wire rack and let cool.

4 To make the frosting, put all the ingredients in a heatproof bowl set over a saucepan of simmering water. Using an electric mixer, beat for 5–6 minutes, until the mixture is thick and holds soft peaks when the mixer is lifted. Swirl the frosting over the cupcakes.

butterscotch cupcakes

MAKES 28

1½ cups all-purpose flour

1 tbsp baking powder

¾ cup unsalted butter, softened

generous ¾ cup light brown sugar

3 eggs, beaten

1 tsp vanilla extract

topping

2 tbsp dark corn syrup

2 tbsp unsalted butter

2 tbsp dark brown sugar

1 Preheat the oven to 375°F/190°C. Put 28 paper liners in a muffin pan or put 28 double-layer paper liners on a baking sheet.

2 Sift the flour and baking powder into a large bowl and add the butter, sugar, eggs, and vanilla extract. Beat well until the mixture is smooth.

3 Divide the batter among the paper liners. Bake in the preheated oven for 15–20 minutes, or until risen, firm, and golden brown. Transfer the cupcakes to a wire rack and let cool.

4 For the topping, put the corn syrup, butter, and sugar into a small pan and heat gently, stirring, until the sugar dissolves. Bring to a boil and cook, stirring, for about 1 minute. Drizzle the topping over the cupcakes and let set.

red velvet cupcakes

MAKES 12

1¼ cups all-purpose flour

1 tsp baking soda

2 tbsp unsweetened cocoa

½ cup butter, softened

¾ cup superfine sugar

1 extra large egg, beaten

½ cup buttermilk

1 tsp vanilla extract

1 tbsp red liquid food coloring

red colored sugar or red sugar sprinkles, to decorate

frosting

⅔ cup cream cheese

6 tbsp unsalted butter, softened

2½ cups confectioners' sugar, sifted

1 Preheat the oven to 350°F/180°C. Put 12 paper liners in a muffin pan or put 12 double-layer paper liners on a baking sheet.

2 Sift together the flour, baking soda, and cocoa. Put the butter and sugar in a bowl and beat together until pale and creamy. Gradually beat in the egg and half of the flour mixture. Beat in the buttermilk, vanilla extract, and food coloring. Fold in the remaining flour mixture. Spoon the batter into the paper liners.

3 Bake the cupcakes for 15–20 minutes, until risen and firm to the touch. Transfer to a wire rack and let cool.

4 To make the frosting, put the cream cheese and butter in a bowl and blend together with a spatula. Beat in the confectioners' sugar until smooth and creamy. Pipe or swirl the frosting on the top of the cupcakes. Sprinkle with the red sugar or sugar sprinkles.

Step 3

Step 4

Step 4

fudge & raisin cupcakes

MAKES 10

4 oz/115 g vanilla fudge, cut into small chunks

1 tbsp milk

6 tbsp butter, softened

3 tbsp light brown sugar

1 extra large egg, lightly beaten

¾ cup self-rising flour

3 tbsp raisins

1 Preheat the oven to 375°F/190°C. Put 10 paper liners in a muffin pan or put 10 double-layer paper liners on a baking sheet.

2 Put half of the fudge in a heatproof bowl with the milk and set over a saucepan of gently simmering water until the fudge has melted. Remove from the heat and stir until smooth. Let cool for 10 minutes.

3 Put the butter and sugar into a bowl and beat together until light and fluffy. Gradually beat in the egg. Sift in the flour and, using a metal spoon, fold gently into the mixture with the raisins. Fold in the melted fudge. Spoon the batter into the paper liners. Scatter the remaining fudge chunks over the cupcakes.

4 Bake the cupcakes in the preheated oven for 15–20 minutes, or until risen and golden brown. Transfer to a wire rack and let cool.

drizzled honey cupcakes

MAKES 12

generous ½ cup self-rising flour

¼ tsp ground cinnamon

pinch of ground cloves

pinch of grated nutmeg

6 tbsp butter, softened

scant ½ cup superfine sugar

1 tbsp honey

finely grated rind of 1 orange

2 eggs, lightly beaten

¾ cup chopped walnut pieces

topping

2 tbsp chopped walnuts

¼ tsp ground cinnamon

2 tbsp honey

juice of 1 orange

1 Preheat the oven to 375°F/190°C. Put 12 paper liners in a muffin pan, or put 12 double-layer paper liners on a baking sheet.

2 Sift the flour, cinnamon, cloves, and nutmeg together into a bowl. Put the butter and sugar in a separate bowl and beat together until light and fluffy. Beat in the honey and orange rind, then gradually add the eggs, beating well after each addition. Using a metal spoon, fold in the flour mixture. Stir in the walnuts, then spoon the batter into the paper liners.

3 Bake the cupcakes in the preheated oven for 20 minutes, or until well risen and golden brown. Transfer to a wire rack and let cool.

4 To make the topping, mix together the walnuts and cinnamon. Put the honey and orange juice in a pan and heat gently, stirring, until combined.

5 When the cupcakes have almost cooled, prick the tops all over with a fork or skewer and then drizzle with the warm honey mixture. Sprinkle the walnut topping over the top of each cupcake and serve warm or cold.

hot marmalade cupcakes

MAKES 4

1 small orange

6 tbsp butter, softened, plus extra for greasing

scant ½ cup superfine sugar

1 extra large egg, lightly beaten

generous ¾ cup self-rising flour

2 tbsp fine shred marmalade, warmed

crème fraîche or whipped heavy cream, to serve

1 Put the orange in a saucepan and cover with water. Bring to a boil, then reduce the heat, cover, and simmer for 1 hour, until soft. Remove the orange from the water and let cool for 30 minutes.

2 Preheat the oven to 350°F/180°C. Grease four ¾-cup ovenproof dishes (such as ramekins) with butter.

3 Cut the orange into chunks and remove any seeds. Put all the orange chunks (rind included) into a food processor and blend until finely minced. Add the butter, sugar, egg, and flour and process until well blended. Spoon the batter into the dishes.

4 Put the dishes on a baking sheet and bake in the preheated oven for 25–30 minutes, or until risen, firm, and golden brown. Cool for 2–3 minutes, then brush the warm marmalade over the top of each cupcake. Serve with crème fraîche or whipped heavy cream.

queen cupcakes

MAKES 18

½ cup butter, softened

generous ½ cup superfine sugar

2 extra large eggs, lightly beaten

4 tsp lemon juice

scant 1¼ cups self-rising flour

¾ cup currants

2–4 tbsp milk, if necessary

1 Preheat the oven to 375°F/190°C. Put 18 paper liners in 2 muffin pans or put 18 double-layer paper liners on 2 baking sheets.

2 Put the butter and sugar in a bowl and beat together until light and fluffy. Gradually beat in the eggs, then beat in the lemon juice with 1 tablespoon of the flour. Using a metal spoon, fold in the remaining flour and the currants, adding a little milk, if necessary, to give a soft dropping consistency. Spoon the batter into the paper liners.

3 Bake the cupcakes in the preheated oven for 15–20 minutes, or until well risen and golden brown. Transfer to a wire rack and let cool.

Step 2

Step 2

Step 3

earl grey cupcakes

MAKES 10

1½ cups all-purpose flour

1 tbsp baking powder

½ tsp apple pie spice

¾ cup unsalted butter, softened

generous ¾ cup superfine sugar

3 eggs, beaten

1 tsp vanilla extract

2 tbsp strong Earl Grey tea

¼ cup currants

confectioners' sugar and apple pie spice, for dusting

1 Preheat the oven to 350°F/180°C. Put ten 1-cup ovenproof dishes (such as ramekins) onto baking sheets.

2 Sift the flour, baking powder, and apple pie spice into a large bowl and add the butter, superfine sugar, eggs, and vanilla extract. Beat well until the mixture is smooth, then stir in the tea and half of the currants.

3 Divide the batter among the cups and sprinkle with the remaining currants. Bake in the preheated oven for 20–25 minutes, or until risen, firm, and golden brown. Turn out the cupcakes onto a wire rack and let cool.

4 To serve, dust the cupcakes with a little confectioners' sugar and apple pie spice.

sugar & spice cupcakes

MAKES 14

½ **cup butter, softened**

½ **cup superfine sugar**

2 eggs, lightly beaten

generous ¾ cup self-rising flour

2 tsp ground allspice

¼ **cup mixed peel**

⅓ **cup chopped candied cherries**

1 tbsp milk

4 white sugar cubes, coarsely crushed

glaze

2 tbsp granulated sugar

3 tbsp water

1 Preheat the oven to 375°F/190°C. Put 14 paper liners in 2 muffin pans or put 14 double-layer paper liners on a baking sheet.

2 Put the butter and sugar in a bowl and beat together until light and fluffy. Gradually beat in the eggs. Sift in the flour and half of the allspice and, using a metal spoon, fold gently into the mixture with the mixed peel, cherries, and milk. Spoon the batter into the paper liners.

3 Mix together the crushed sugar cubes and remaining allspice and sprinkle over the top of the cupcakes.

4 Bake the cupcakes in the preheated oven for 15–20 minutes, or until risen and firm to touch. Transfer to a wire rack.

5 To make the glaze, place the sugar and water in a small pan and heat until the sugar dissolves. Bring to a boil and boil, without stirring, for 2–3 minutes, until reduced and syrupy. Brush the hot syrup over the warm cupcakes. Let cool.

jelly cupcakes

MAKES 28

1½ cups all-purpose flour

1 tbsp baking powder

1 tbsp cornstarch

¾ cup unsalted butter, softened

generous ¾ cup superfine sugar

3 eggs, beaten

1 tsp vanilla extract

¼ cup raspberry jelly

confectioners' sugar, for dusting

1 Preheat the oven to 375°F/190°C. Put 28 paper liners into shallow muffin pans or put double-layer paper liners onto baking sheets.

2 Sift the flour, baking powder, and cornstarch into a large bowl and add the butter, superfine sugar, eggs, and vanilla extract. Beat well until the mixture is smooth.

3 Divide the batter among the paper liners and put about ½ teaspoon of jelly onto the center of each, without pressing down.

4 Bake in the preheated oven for 15–20 minutes, or until risen, firm, and golden brown. Transfer the cupcakes to a wire rack and let cool. Dust with the confectioners' sugar before serving.

frosted peanut butter cupcakes

MAKES 16

4 tbsp butter, softened

1¼ cups brown sugar

generous ⅓ cup chunky peanut butter

2 eggs, lightly beaten

1 tsp vanilla extract

1½ cups all-purpose flour

2 tsp baking powder

generous ⅓ cup milk

chopped peanuts, to decorate

frosting

scant 1 cup cream cheese

2 tbsp butter, softened

2 cups confectioners' sugar

1 Preheat the oven to 350°F/180°C. Put 16 paper liners into 2 shallow muffin pans or put 16 double-layer paper liners on a large baking sheet.

2 Put the butter, sugar, and peanut butter in a bowl and beat together for 1–2 minutes, or until well mixed. Gradually add the eggs, beating well after each addition, then add the vanilla extract. Sift in the flour and baking powder and then, using a metal spoon, fold them into the mixture, alternating with the milk. Spoon the batter into the paper liners. Bake the cupcakes in the preheated oven for 25 minutes, or until well risen and golden brown. Transfer to a wire rack and let cool.

3 To make the frosting, put the cream cheese and butter in a large bowl and, using an electric mixer, beat together until smooth. Sift the confectioners' sugar into the mixture, then beat together until well mixed. When the cupcakes are cold, pipe a swirl on top of each cupcake and decorate with the peanuts. Store the cupcakes in the refrigerator until ready to serve.

Step 2

Step 2

Step 3

chewy oatmeal-topped cupcakes

MAKES 8

3 tbsp soft margarine

3 tbsp raw brown sugar

1 tbsp dark corn syrup

⅔ cup rolled oats

4 tbsp butter, softened

¼ cup superfine sugar

1 extra large egg, lightly beaten

generous ⅓ cup self-rising flour

1 Preheat the oven to 375°F/190°C. Put 8 paper liners in a muffin pan or put 8 double-layer paper liners on a baking sheet.

2 Place the margarine, raw brown sugar, and corn syrup in a small saucepan and heat gently until the margarine has melted. Stir in the oats. Set aside.

3 Put the butter and superfine sugar in a bowl and beat together until light and fluffy. Gradually beat in the egg. Sift in the flour and, using a metal spoon, fold gently into the mixture. Spoon the batter into the paper liners. Gently spoon the oatmeal mixture over the top.

4 Bake the cupcakes in the preheated oven for 20 minutes, or until golden brown. Transfer to a wire rack and let cool.

cherry & almond cupcakes

MAKES 4

4 tbsp butter, softened, plus extra for greasing

¼ cup superfine sugar

1 extra large egg, lightly beaten

generous ⅓ cup self-rising flour

scant ½ cup ground almonds

½ tsp almond extract

1 tbsp milk

¼ cup quartered candied cherries

1 tbsp toasted slivered almonds, to decorate

icing

⅓ cup confectioners' sugar

2 tsp lemon juice

1 Preheat the oven to 350°F/180°C. Grease four 1-cup ovenproof dishes (such as ramekins) with butter.

2 Put the butter and sugar in a bowl and beat together until light and fluffy. Gradually beat in the egg. Sift in the flour and, using a metal spoon, fold into the mixture with the ground almonds, almond extract, and milk. Spoon the batter into the dishes. Scatter over the cherries.

3 Put the dishes on a baking sheet and bake in the preheated oven for 25–30 minutes, or until risen, firm, and golden brown. Let cool.

4 To make the icing, sift the confectioners' sugar into a bowl and stir in the lemon juice to make a smooth icing. Using a teaspoon, drizzle the icing over the cupcakes and decorate with slivered almonds. Let set.

gingerbread cupcakes

MAKES 30

1½ cups all-purpose flour

1 tbsp baking powder

2 tsp ground ginger

1 tsp ground cinnamon

¾ cup unsalted butter, softened

generous ¾ cup dark brown sugar

3 eggs, beaten

1 tsp vanilla extract

chopped candied ginger, to decorate

frosting

6 tbsp unsalted butter, softened

1⅓ cups confectioners' sugar, sifted

3 tbsp orange juice

1 Preheat the oven to 375°F/190°C. Put 30 paper liners into shallow muffin pans or put double-layer paper liners onto baking sheets.

2 Sift the flour, baking powder, ginger, and cinnamon into a large bowl and add the butter, sugar, eggs, and vanilla extract. Beat well until the mixture is smooth.

3 Divide the batter among the paper liners. Bake in the preheated oven for 15–20 minutes, or until risen, firm, and golden brown. Transfer the cupcakes to a wire rack and let cool.

4 For the frosting, beat together the butter, confectioners' sugar, and orange juice until smooth. Spoon a little frosting on top of each cupcake and top with candied ginger.

marzipan chunk cupcakes

MAKES 32

1½ cups all-purpose flour

2 tsp cornstarch

1 tbsp baking powder

¾ cup unsalted butter, softened

generous ¾ cup superfine sugar

3 eggs, beaten

1 tsp almond extract

3 oz/85 g golden marzipan, cut into ¼-inch/ 5-mm dice

1 Preheat the oven to 375°F/190°C. Put 32 paper liners into shallow muffin pans or put double-layer paper liners onto baking sheets.

2 Sift the flour, cornstarch, and baking powder into a large bowl and add the butter, sugar, eggs, and almond extract. Beat well until the mixture is smooth.

3 Divide the batter among the paper liners and sprinkle a few pieces of marzipan on top of each. Bake in the preheated oven for 15–20 minutes, or until risen, firm, and golden brown. Transfer the cupcakes to a wire rack and let cool.

VARIATION

To add a vanilla frosting to the cupcakes, beat together 5½ oz/150 g unsalted butter, 10½ oz/300 g confectioners' sugar and ½ tsp vanilla extract until smooth. Spread or pipe the frosting on top of each cake.

2

Dreamy Chocolate

chocolate-topped cupcakes

MAKES 30

1½ **cups all-purpose flour**

1 **tbsp baking powder**

¾ **cup unsalted butter, softened**

generous ¾ **cup superfine sugar**

3 **eggs, beaten**

1 **tsp vanilla extract**

2 **tbsp milk**

1 **tbsp unsweetened cocoa**

½ **cup grated milk chocolate**

3 **tbsp apricot jelly, warmed**

1 Preheat the oven to 375°F/190°C. Put 30 paper liners into shallow muffin pans or put double-layer paper liners onto baking sheets.

2 Sift the flour and baking powder into a large bowl and add the butter, sugar, eggs, and vanilla extract. Beat well until the mixture is smooth. Combine the milk and cocoa and stir into the mix.

3 Divide the batter among the paper liners and sprinkle with 2 tablespoons of the grated chocolate. Bake in the preheated oven for 15–20 minutes, or until risen, firm, and golden brown. Transfer the cupcakes to a wire rack and let cool.

4 When the cupcakes are cold, brush the tops with the apricot jelly and sprinkle with the remaining grated chocolate.

chocolate butterfly cupcakes

MAKES 12

½ **cup soft margarine**

½ **cup superfine sugar**

1½ **cups self-rising flour**

2 **extra large eggs**

2 **tbsp unsweetened cocoa**

1 **oz/25 g semisweet chocolate, melted**

confectioners' sugar, for dusting

buttercream filling

6 **tbsp unsalted butter, softened**

1½ **cups confectioners' sugar**

1 **oz/25 g semisweet chocolate, melted**

1 Preheat the oven to 350°F/180°C. Put 12 paper liners in a muffin pan or put 12 double-layer paper liners on a baking sheet.

2 Put the margarine, sugar, flour, eggs, and cocoa in a large bowl and, using a electric mixer, beat together until just smooth. Beat in the melted chocolate. Spoon the batter into the paper liners, filling them three-quarters full.

3 Bake the cupcakes in the preheated oven for 15 minutes, or until springy to the touch. Transfer to a wire rack and let cool.

4 To make the filling, put the butter in a bowl and beat until fluffy. Sift in the confectioners' sugar and beat together until smooth. Add the melted chocolate and beat together until well mixed.

5 When the cupcakes are cooled, use a serrated knife to cut a circle from the top of each cake and then cut each circle in half. Spread or pipe a little of the filling into the center of each cupcake and press the 2 semicircular halves into it at an angle to resemble butterfly wings. Dust with sifted confectioners' sugar before serving.

molten-centered chocolate cupcakes

MAKES 8

4 tbsp soft margarine

½ cup superfine sugar

1 extra large egg

½ cup self-rising flour

1 tbsp unsweetened cocoa

2 oz/55 g semisweet chocolate

confectioners' sugar, for dusting

1 Preheat the oven to 375°F/190°C. Put 8 paper liners in a muffin pan or put 8 double-layer paper liners on a baking sheet.

2 Put the margarine, sugar, egg, flour, and cocoa in a large bowl and, using a electric mixer, beat together until just smooth.

3 Spoon half of the batter into the paper liners. Using a teaspoon, make an indentation in the center of each cake. Break the chocolate evenly into 8 squares and place a piece in each indentation, then spoon the remaining cake batter on top.

4 Bake the cupcakes in the preheated oven for 20 minutes, or until well risen and springy to the touch. Let the cupcakes cool for 2–3 minutes before serving warm, dusted with sifted confectioners' sugar.

frosted chocolate cupcakes

MAKES 14

½ cup butter, softened

generous ½ cup superfine sugar

2 extra large eggs, beaten

1 cup self-rising flour, sifted

½ tsp baking powder

1½ tbsp unsweetened cocoa, sifted

2 oz/55 g semisweet chocolate, melted

chocolate shapes and edible gold dagrées, to decorate

frosting

5½ oz/150 g semisweet chocolate, chopped

scant 1 cup heavy cream

⅔ cup unsalted butter, softened

2½ cups confectioners' sugar, sifted

1 Preheat the oven to 350°F/180°C. Put 14 paper liners in a muffin pan or put 14 double-layer paper liners on a large baking sheet.

2 Put the butter, sugar, eggs, flour, baking powder, and cocoa in a bowl and using an electric whisk, beat together until pale and creamy. Fold in the melted chocolate. Spoon the batter into the paper liners. Bake the cupcakes for 15–20 minutes, until risen and firm to the touch. Transfer to a wire rack and let cool.

3 To make the frosting, put the chocolate in a heatproof bowl. Heat the cream in a pan until boiling, then pour it over the chocolate and stir until smooth. Let cool for 20 minutes, stirring occasionally, until thickened. Put the butter in a bowl and gradually beat in the confectioners' sugar until smooth. Beat in the chocolate mixture. Chill for 15–20 minutes. Spoon the frosting into a pastry bag fitted with a large star tip and pipe swirls on top of each cake. Decorate with chocolate shapes and gold balls.

Step 2

Step 2

Step 3

double chocolate cupcakes

MAKES 18

3 oz/85 g white chocolate

1 tbsp milk

generous ¾ cup self-rising flour

½ tsp baking powder

½ cup butter, softened

generous ½ cup superfine sugar

2 eggs

1 tsp vanilla extract

topping

5 oz/140 g milk chocolate

18 white chocolate disk

1 Preheat the oven to 375°F/190°C. Put 18 paper liners in 2 muffin pans or put 18 double-layer paper liners on a large baking sheet.

2 Break the white chocolate into a heatproof bowl and add the milk. Set the bowl over a saucepan of simmering water and heat until melted. Remove from the heat and stir gently until smooth.

3 Sift the flour and baking powder into a bowl. Add the butter, sugar, eggs, and vanilla extract and, using an electric mixer, beat together until smooth. Fold in the melted white chocolate. Spoon the batter into the paper liners.

4 Bake in the preheated oven for 20 minutes, or until risen and golden brown. Transfer to a wire rack and let cool.

5 To make the topping, break the chocolate into a heatproof bowl and set the bowl over a saucepan of gently simmering water until melted. Cool for 5 minutes, then spread over the top of the cupcakes. Decorate each cupcake with a chocolate disk.

chocolate brownie cupcakes

MAKES 12

8 oz/225 g semisweet chocolate, broken into pieces

6 tbsp butter

2 extra large eggs

1 cup dark brown sugar

1 tsp vanilla extract

1 cup all-purpose flour

¾ cup chopped walnuts

1 Preheat the oven to 350°F/180°C. Put 12 paper liners in a muffin pan or put 12 double-layer paper liners on a baking sheet.

2 Place the chocolate and butter in a saucepan and heat gently, stirring continuously, until melted. Remove from the heat and stir until smooth. Let cool slightly.

3 Place the eggs and sugar in a large bowl and beat together, then add the vanilla extract. Sift in the flour and stir until mixed together, then stir the melted chocolate into the mixture until combined. Stir in the chopped walnuts. Spoon the batter into the paper liners.

4 Bake in the preheated oven for 30 minutes, or until firm to the touch but still slightly moist in the center. Let the cupcakes cool for 10 minutes, then transfer to a wire rack and let cool completely.

devil's food cupcakes

MAKES 18

3½ tbsp soft margarine

generous ½ cup brown sugar

2 extra large eggs

¾ cup all-purpose flour

½ tsp baking soda

¼ cup unsweetened cocoa

½ cup sour cream

frosting

4½ oz/125 g semisweet chocolate

2 tbsp superfine sugar

⅔ cup sour cream

chocolate caraque, to decorate

1 Preheat the oven to 350°F/180°C. Put 18 paper liners in 2 muffin pans or put 18 double-layer paper liners on 2 baking sheets.

2 Put the margarine, sugar, eggs, flour, baking soda, and cocoa in a large bowl and, using a electric mixer, beat together until just smooth. Using a metal spoon, fold in the sour cream. Spoon the batter into the paper liners.

3 Bake the cupcakes in the preheated oven for 20 minutes, or until well risen and firm to the touch. Transfer to a wire rack and let cool.

4 To make the frosting, break the chocolate into a heatproof bowl. Set the bowl over a saucepan of gently simmering water and heat until melted, stirring occasionally. Remove from the heat and let cool slightly, then beat in the sugar and sour cream until combined. Spread the frosting over the tops of the cupcakes and let set in the refrigerator before serving. Serve decorated with chocolate caraque.

chocolate curl cupcakes

MAKES 18

6 tbsp unsalted butter, softened

½ cup superfine sugar

2 eggs, lightly beaten

2 tbsp milk

⅓ cup semisweet chocolate chips

1½ cups self-rising flour

¼ cup unsweetened cocoa

chocolate curls, to decorate

frosting

8 oz/225 g white chocolate

⅔ cup low-fat cream cheese

1 Preheat the oven to 400°F/200°C. Put 18 paper liners in 2 muffin pans or put 18 double-layer paper liners on 2 baking sheets.

2 Put the butter and sugar in a bowl and beat together until light and fluffy. Gradually add the eggs, beating well after each addition. Add the milk, then fold in the chocolate chips. Sift the flour and cocoa, then fold into the mixture. Spoon the batter into the paper liners and smooth the tops.

3 Bake the cupcakes in the preheated oven for 20 minutes, or until well risen and springy to the touch. Transfer to a wire rack and let cool.

4 To make the frosting, break the chocolate into a small heatproof bowl and set the bowl over a saucepan of gently simmering water until melted. Let cool slightly. Put the cream cheese in a bowl and beat until softened, then beat in the slightly cooled chocolate. Spread a little of the frosting over the top of each cupcake, then let chill in the refrigerator for 1 hour before serving. Decorate with chocolate curls.

Step 2

Step 4

Step 4

chocolate & sponge toffee cupcakes

MAKES 30

1½ cups all-purpose flour

1 tbsp baking powder

¾ cup unsalted butter, softened

generous ¾ cup superfine sugar

3 eggs, beaten

1 tsp vanilla extract

1½ oz/40 g chocolate-covered sponge toffee, finely chopped

topping

1¾ cups confectioners' sugar, sifted

2 tsp unsweetened cocoa

about 2 tbsp water

1½ oz/40 g chocolate-covered sponge toffee, cut into chunks

1 Preheat the oven to 375°F/190°C. Put 30 paper liners into shallow muffin pans or put 30 double-layer liners onto baking sheets.

2 Sift the flour and baking powder into a large bowl and add the butter, superfine sugar, eggs, and vanilla extract. Beat well until the mixture is smooth, then stir in the chopped sponge toffee.

3 Divide the batter among the paper liners. Bake in the preheated oven for 15–20 minutes, or until risen, firm, and golden brown. Transfer the cupcakes to a wire rack and let cool.

4 For the topping, combine the confectioners' sugar, cocoa, and water into a smooth paste. Spoon a little on top of each cupcake and top with chunks of sponge toffee. Let set.

rocky road cupcakes

MAKES 12

2 tbsp unsweetened cocoa

2 tbsp hot water

½ cup butter, softened

½ cup superfine sugar

2 eggs, lightly beaten

generous ¾ cup self-rising flour

topping

¼ cup chopped mixed nuts

3½ oz/100 g milk chocolate, melted

2 cups miniature marshmallows

¼ cup chopped candied cherries

1 Preheat the oven to 350°F/180°C. Put 12 paper liners in a muffin pan or put 12 double-layer paper liners on a baking sheet.

2 Blend the cocoa and hot water together and set aside. Put the butter and sugar in a bowl and beat together until light and fluffy. Gradually beat in the eggs, then beat in the blended cocoa. Sift in the flour and, using a metal spoon, fold gently into the batter. Spoon the mixture into the paper liners.

3 Bake the cupcakes in the preheated oven for 20 minutes, or until risen and firm to the touch. Transfer to a wire rack and let cool.

4 To make the topping, stir the nuts into the melted chocolate and spread a little of the mixture over the top of the cakes. Lightly stir the marshmallows and cherries into the remaining chocolate mixture and pile on top of the cupcakes. Let set.

dark & white cupcakes

MAKES 20

scant 1 cup water

6 tbsp butter

scant ½ cup superfine sugar

1 tbsp corn syrup

3 tbsp milk

1 tsp vanilla extract

1 tsp baking soda

1½ cups cups all-purpose flour

2 tbsp unsweetened cocoa

semisweet and white chocolate curls, to decorate

topping

1¾ oz/50 g semisweet chocolate

4 tbsp water

3½ tbsp butter

1¾ oz/50 g white chocolate

3 cups confectioners' sugar

1 Preheat the oven to 350°F/180°C. Put 20 paper liners in 2 muffin pans or put 20 double-layer paper liners on 2 baking sheets.

2 Put the water, butter, superfine sugar, and corn syrup in a pan. Heat gently, stirring, until the sugar has dissolved, then bring to a boil. Reduce the heat and cook gently for 5 minutes. Remove from the heat and let cool.

3 Meanwhile, put the milk and vanilla extract in a bowl. Add the baking soda and stir to dissolve. Sift the flour and cocoa into a separate bowl and add the syrup mixture. Stir in the milk mixture and beat until smooth. Spoon the batter into the paper liners until they are two-thirds full.

4 Bake the cupcakes in the preheated oven for 20 minutes, or until well risen and firm to the touch. Transfer to a wire rack and let cool.

5 To make the topping, break the semisweet chocolate into a small heatproof bowl, add half of the water and half of the butter, and set the bowl over a pan of gently simmering water until melted. Stir until smooth and let stand over the water. Using another bowl, repeat with the white chocolate and remaining water and butter. Sift half of the confectioners' sugar into each bowl and beat until smooth and thick. Top half of the cupcakes with the white chocolate icing and scatter over the semisweet chocolate curls, then top the remaining cupcakes with the semisweet chocolate icing and white chocolate curls. Let set.

white chocolate & rose cupcakes

MAKES 12

½ **cup unsalted butter**

generous ½ cup superfine sugar

1 tsp rose water

2 eggs, beaten

1 cup self-rising flour

¼ **cup grated white chocolate**

sugar-frosted pink rose petals, to decorate

frosting

4 oz/115 g white chocolate, broken into pieces

2 tbsp milk

soft cheese, such as cream cheese, ricotta, or mascarpone

¼ **cup confectioners' sugar, sifted**

1 Preheat the oven to 350°F/180°C. Put 12 paper liners in a muffin pan or put 12 double-layer liners on a large baking sheet.

2 Put the butter, sugar, and rose water in a bowl and beat together until pale and creamy. Gradually beat in the eggs. Sift over the flour and fold in gently. Fold in the white chocolate. Spoon the batter into the paper liners.

3 Bake the cupcakes for 15–20 minutes, until risen and firm to the touch. Transfer to a wire rack and let cool.

4 To make the frosting, put the chocolate and milk in a heatproof bowl set over a pan of simmering water and melt. Remove from the heat and stir until smooth. Let cool for 30 minutes. Put the soft cheese and confectioners' sugar in a bowl and beat together until smooth and creamy. Fold in the chocolate. Chill in the refrigerator for 1 hour. Swirl the frosting over the top of the cupcakes. Decorate with the sugar-frosted rose petals.

Step 3

Step 4

Step 4

peppermint cupcakes

MAKES 32

1½ cups all-purpose flour

1 tbsp baking powder

¾ cup unsalted butter, softened

generous ¾ cup superfine sugar

3 eggs, beaten

1 tsp peppermint extract

scant ½ cup semisweet chocolate chips

topping

3½ oz/100 g semisweet chocolate, melted

10 mint chocolate sticks, broken into short lengths

1 Preheat the oven to 375°F/190°C. Put 32 paper liners into shallow muffin pans or put 32 double-layer liners onto baking sheets.

2 Sift the flour and baking powder into a large bowl and add the butter, sugar, eggs, and peppermint extract. Beat well until the mixture is smooth, then stir in half of the chocolate chips.

3 Divide the batter among the paper liners and sprinkle with the remaining chocolate chips. Bake in the preheated oven for 15–20 minutes, or until risen, firm, and golden brown. Transfer the cupcakes to a wire rack and let cool.

4 When cooled, drizzle the cakes with the melted chocolate and decorate with pieces of chocolate mint sticks. Let set.

chocolate & hazelnut cupcakes

MAKES 18

¾ cup butter, softened

generous ½ cup light brown sugar

2 extra large eggs, lightly beaten

2 tbsp chocolate-and-hazelnut spread

1¼ cups self-rising flour

scant ½ cup blanched hazelnuts, coarsely ground

topping

5 tbsp chocolate-and-hazelnut spread

18 whole blanched hazelnuts

1 Preheat the oven to 350°F/180°C. Put 18 paper liners in 2 muffin pans or put 18 double-layer paper liners on a large baking sheet.

2 Put the butter and sugar in a mixing bowl and beat together until light and fluffy. Gradually beat in the eggs, then stir in the chocolate-and-hazelnut spread. Sift in the flour and, using a metal spoon, fold into the mixture with the ground hazelnuts. Spoon the batter into the paper liners.

3 Bake the cupcakes in the preheated oven for 20–25 minutes, or until risen and firm to the touch. Transfer to a wire rack and let cool.

4 When the cupcakes are cold, swirl some chocolate-and-hazelnut spread over the top of each cupcake and top with a hazelnut.

hot pecan brownie cupcakes

MAKES 6

4 oz/115 g dark chocolate, broken into pieces

½ cup butter, plus extra for greasing

2 eggs

generous ½ cup light brown sugar

3 tbsp maple syrup

generous ¾ cup all-purpose flour, sifted

½ cup chopped pecans

1 Preheat the oven to 350°F/180°C. Grease six ¾-cup ovenproof dishes (such as ramekins) with butter.

2 Put the chocolate and butter into a heatproof bowl set over a saucepan of gently simmering water until melted, stirring occasionally. Cool for 5 minutes.

3 Put the eggs, sugar, and maple syrup in a bowl and beat together until well blended. Beat in the chocolate mixture, then fold in the flour and two-thirds of the pecans. Pour the batter into the dishes and scatter over the rest of the nuts.

4 Put the dishes on a baking sheet and bake in the preheated oven for 25–30 minutes, or until the cupcakes have risen and are crisp on top but still feel slightly wobbly if lightly pressed. Serve hot.

mocha cupcakes

MAKES 20

**2 tbsp instant espresso
coffee powder**

6 tbsp unsalted butter

6 tbsp superfine sugar

1 tbsp honey

scant 1 cup water

1½ cups all-purpose flour

2 tbsp unsweetened cocoa

1 tsp baking soda

3 tbsp milk

**1 extra large egg, lightly
beaten**

topping

1 cup heavy cream

**unsweetened cocoa, sifted,
for dusting**

1 Preheat the oven to 350°F/180°C. Put 20 paper liners in 2 muffin pans or put 20 double-layer paper liners on 2 baking sheets.

2 Put the coffee powder, butter, sugar, honey, and water in a saucepan and heat gently, stirring, until the sugar has dissolved. Bring to a boil, then reduce the heat and let simmer for 5 minutes. Pour into a large heatproof bowl and let cool.

3 When the mixture has cooled, sift in the flour and cocoa. Dissolve the baking soda in the milk, then add to the mixture with the egg and beat together until smooth. Spoon the batter into the paper liners. Bake the cupcakes in the preheated oven for 15–20 minutes, or until well risen and firm to the touch. Transfer to a wire rack and let cool.

4 For the topping, whip the cream in a bowl until it holds its shape. Just before serving, spoon generous teaspoonfuls of the whipped cream on top of each cake, then dust lightly with the sifted cocoa.

Step
2

Step
3

Step
4

chocolate & orange cupcakes

MAKES 16

½ **cup butter, softened**

generous ½ **cup superfine sugar**

finely grated rind and juice of ½ orange

2 eggs, lightly beaten

generous ¾ **cup self-rising flour**

3 tbsp grated semisweet chocolate

frosting

4 oz /115 g semisweet chocolate, broken into pieces

2 tbsp unsalted butter

l tbsp light corn syrup

thin strips candied orange peel, to decorate

1 Preheat the oven to 350°F/180°C. Put 16 paper liners in 2 muffin pans or put 16 double-layer paper liners on a baking sheet.

2 Put the butter, sugar, and orange rind in a bowl and beat together until light and fluffy. Gradually beat in the eggs. Sift in the flour and, using a metal spoon, fold gently into the mixture with the orange juice and grated chocolate. Spoon the batter into the paper liners.

3 Bake the cupcakes in the preheated oven for 20 minutes, or until risen and golden brown. Transfer to a wire rack and let cool.

4 To make the frosting, break the chocolate into a heatproof bowl and add the butter and corn syrup. Set the bowl over a saucepan of simmering water and heat until melted. Remove from the heat and stir until smooth. Cool until the frosting is thick enough to spread. Spread over the cupcakes and decorate each cupcake with a few strips of candied orange peel. Let set.

chocolate & cherry cupcakes

MAKES 12

3 oz/75 g semisweet chocolate

1 tsp lemon juice

4 tbsp milk

generous 1 cup self-rising flour

1 tbsp unsweetened cocoa

½ tsp baking soda

2 eggs

4 tbsp butter, softened

generous ½ cup light brown sugar

3 tbsp chopped dried and sweetened sour cherries

2 tbsp cherry liqueur (optional)

⅔ cup heavy cream, softly whipped

5 tbsp cherry conserve

unsweetened cocoa, to dust

1 Preheat the oven to 350°F/180°C. Put 12 paper liners in a muffin pan or put 12 double-layer paper liners on a baking sheet.

2 Break the chocolate into a heatproof bowl and set the bowl over a saucepan of gently simmering water until melted. Add the lemon juice to the milk and let stand for 10 minutes—the milk will curdle a little.

3 Sift the flour, cocoa, and baking soda into a bowl. Add the eggs, butter, sugar, and milk mixture and beat with an electric mixer until smooth. Fold in the melted chocolate and cherries. Spoon the batter into the paper liners.

4 Bake the cupcakes in the preheated oven for 20–25 minutes, until risen and firm to the touch. Transfer to a wire rack and let cool.

5 When the cupcakes are cold, use a serrated knife to cut a circle from the top of each cupcake. Sprinkle the cakes with a little cherry liqueur, if using. Spoon the whipped cream into the centers and top with a small spoonful of conserve. Gently replace the cupcake tops and dust lightly with cocoa. Store in the refrigerator until ready to serve.

pear & chocolate cupcakes

MAKES 12

½ **cup margarine**

generous ½ **cup light brown sugar**

2 **eggs**

¾ **cup self-rising flour**

½ **tsp baking powder**

2 **tbsp unsweetened cocoa**

4 **canned pear halves, drained and sliced**

2 **tbsp honey, warmed**

1 Preheat the oven to 375°F/190°C. Put 12 paper liners in a muffin pan or put 12 double-layer paper liners on a baking sheet.

2 Put the margarine, sugar, eggs, flour, baking powder, and cocoa in a large bowl and, using an electric mixer, beat together until just smooth. Spoon the batter into the paper liners and smooth the tops. Arrange 2 pear slices on top of each cupcake.

3 Bake the cupcakes in the preheated oven for 20 minutes, or until risen and just firm to the touch. Transfer to a wire cooling rack. While the cupcakes are still warm, glaze with the honey. Let cool completely.

chocolate chip cupcakes

MAKES 8

scant ½ cup soft margarine

½ cup superfine sugar

2 extra large eggs

scant ¾ cup self-rising flour

½ cup semisweet chocolate chips

1 Preheat the oven to 375°F/190°C. Put 8 muffin paper liners in a muffin pan or put 8 double-layer paper liners on a baking sheet.

2 Put the margarine, sugar, eggs, and flour in a large bowl and, using a electric mixer, beat together until just smooth. Fold in the chocolate chips and spoon the batter into the paper liners.

3 Bake the cupcakes in the preheated oven for 20–25 minutes, or until well risen and golden brown. Transfer to a wire rack and let cool.

Step 2

Step 2

Step 3

white chocolate chip cupcakes

MAKES 32

1½ cups all-purpose flour

1 tbsp baking powder

¾ cup unsalted butter, softened

generous ¾ cup superfine sugar

3 eggs, beaten

1 tsp vanilla extract

scant ½ cup white chocolate chips

topping

3½ oz/100 g white chocolate, melted

2 tbsp chocolate sprinkles

1 Preheat the oven to 375°F/190°C. Put 32 paper liners into shallow muffin pans or put 32 double-layer liners onto baking sheets.

2 Sift the flour and baking powder into a large bowl and add the butter, sugar, eggs, and vanilla extract. Beat well until the mixture is smooth, then stir in half of the chocolate chips.

3 Divide the batter among the paper liners and sprinkle with the remaining chocolate chips. Bake in the preheated oven for 15–20 minutes, or until risen, firm, and golden brown. Transfer the cupcakes to a wire rack to cool.

4 When the cupcakes are cold, spoon a little melted white chocolate on top of each and decorate with the chocolate sprinkles. Let set.

chocolate fruit & nut cupcakes

MAKES 12

2 oz/55 g semisweet chocolate

6 tbsp butter

1 tbsp dark corn syrup

¼ cup brown sugar

generous ¾ cup self-rising flour

1 extra large egg, beaten

topping

¼ cup chopped candied cherries

¼ cup slivered almonds

1 tbsp raisins

1 tbsp dark corn syrup

1 Preheat the oven to 375°F/190°C. Put 12 paper liners in a muffin pan or put 12 double-layer paper liners on a baking sheet.

2 Put the chocolate, butter, corn syrup, and sugar in a saucepan and heat gently, stirring occasionally, until just melted. Cool for 2 minutes. Sift the flour into a bowl.

3 Pour the chocolate mixture into the bowl. Add the egg and beat until thoroughly blended. Spoon the batter into the paper liners.

4 Mix together the topping ingredients and gently spoon a little of the mixture on top of each cupcake.

5 Bake the cupcakes in the preheated oven for 15–20 minutes, or until risen and firm to the touch. Transfer to a wire rack and let cool.

tiny chocolate cupcakes

MAKES 20

4 tbsp unsalted butter, softened

¼ cup superfine sugar

1 extra large egg, lightly beaten

scant ½ cup self-rising flour

2 tbsp unsweetened cocoa

1 tbsp milk

20 chocolate-coated coffee beans, to decorate

frosting

3½ oz/100 g semisweet chocolate

⅓ cup heavy cream

1 Preheat the oven to 375°F/190°C. Put 20 double-layer mini paper liners on 2 baking sheets.

2 Put the butter and sugar in a bowl and beat together until light and fluffy. Gradually beat in the egg. Sift in the flour and cocoa and then, using a metal spoon, fold them into the mixture. Stir in the milk.

3 Take a pastry bag fitted with a large plain tip, fill it with the batter, and pipe it into the paper liners, filling each one until halfway full.

4 Bake the cakes in the preheated oven for 10–15 minutes, or until well risen and firm to the touch. Transfer to a wire rack and let cool.

5 To make the frosting, break the chocolate into a pan and add the cream. Heat gently, stirring all the time, until the chocolate has melted. Pour into a large heatproof bowl and, using a electric mixer, beat the mixture for 10 minutes, or until thick, glossy, and cool.

6 Take a pastry bag fitted with a large star tip, fill it with the frosting, and pipe a swirl on top of each cupcake. Alternatively, spoon the frosting over the top of each cupcake. Chill in the refrigerator for 1 hour before serving. Serve decorated with a chocolate-coated coffee bean.

marbled chocolate cupcakes

MAKES 21

¾ cup soft margarine

generous ¾ cup superfine sugar

3 eggs

scant 1¼ cups self-rising flour

2 tbsp milk

2 oz/55 g semisweet chocolate, melted

1 Preheat the oven to 350°F/180°C. Put 21 paper liners in 2 muffin pans or put 21 double-layer paper liners on a large baking sheet.

2 Put the margarine, sugar, eggs, flour, and milk in a large bowl and, using an electric mixer, beat together until just smooth.

3 Divide the batter between 2 bowls. Add the melted chocolate to one bowl and stir until well mixed. Using a teaspoon, and alternating the chocolate batter with the plain batter, put four ½-teaspoons into each paper liner.

4 Bake the cupcakes in the preheated oven for 20 minutes, or until well risen and springy to the touch. Transfer to a wire rack and let cool.

VARIATION
Add the grated rind and juice of ½ small orange and a few drops of orange food coloring to the plain cake batter to make marbled chocolate orange cupcakes.

3

Fabulous Fruit & Nut

lemon & raspberry cupcakes

MAKES 12

½ cup butter, softened

generous ½ cup superfine sugar

2 eggs, lightly beaten

generous ¾ cup self-rising flour

finely grated rind of 1 lemon

1 tbsp lemon curd

generous ¾ cup fresh raspberries

topping

2 tbsp butter

1 tbsp light brown sugar

1 tbsp ground almonds

1 tbsp all-purpose flour

1 Preheat the oven to 400°F/200°C. Put 12 paper liners in a muffin pan or put 12 double-layer paper liners on a baking sheet.

2 To make the topping, place the butter in a saucepan and heat gently until melted. Pour into a bowl and add the sugar, ground almonds, and flour and stir together until combined.

3 To make the cupcakes, place the butter and sugar in a large bowl and beat together until light and fluffy, then gradually add the eggs. Sift in the flour and fold into the mixture. Fold in the lemon rind, lemon curd, and raspberries. Spoon the batter into the paper liners. Add the topping to cover the top of each cupcake and press down gently.

4 Bake in the preheated oven for 15–20 minutes, or until golden brown and firm to the touch. Let the cupcakes cool for 10 minutes, then transfer to a wire rack and let cool completely.

lemon butterfly cupcakes

MAKES 12

generous ¾ cup self-rising flour

½ tsp baking powder

½ cup soft margarine

generous ½ cup superfine sugar

2 eggs, lightly beaten

finely grated rind of ½ lemon

2 tbsp milk

confectioners' sugar, for dusting

buttercream filling

6 tbsp butter, softened

1½ cups confectioners' sugar

1 tbsp lemon juice

1 Preheat the oven to 375°F/190°C. Put 12 paper liners in a muffin pan or put 12 double-layer paper liners on a baking sheet.

2 Sift the flour and baking powder into a large bowl. Add the margarine, sugar, eggs, lemon rind, and milk and, using an electric mixer, beat together until smooth. Spoon the batter into the paper liners.

3 Bake the cupcakes in the preheated oven for 15–20 minutes, or until well risen and golden brown. Transfer to a wire rack and let cool.

4 To make the filling, put the butter in a bowl and beat until fluffy. Sift in the confectioners' sugar, add the lemon juice, and beat together until smooth and creamy.

5 When the cupcakes are cold, use a serrated knife to cut a circle from the top of each cupcake and then cut each circle in half. Spread or pipe a little of the filling into the center of the top of each cupcake, then press the 2 semicircular halves into it at an angle to resemble butterfly wings. Dust with sifted confectioners' sugar before serving.

lemon crunch cupcakes

MAKES 12

¾ **cup butter, softened**

generous ¾ cup superfine sugar

1¼ cups self-rising flour

1 tsp baking powder

3 extra large eggs

3 tbsp lemon curd

topping

½ **cup granulated sugar**

juice and grated rind 1 lemon

1 Preheat the oven to 350°F/180°C. Put 12 paper liners in a muffin pan or put 12 double-layer paper liners on a baking sheet.

2 Put the butter, sugar, flour, baking powder, and eggs in a large bowl and, using an electric mixer, beat until the mixture is thoroughly blended. Fold in the lemon curd. Spoon the mixture into the paper liners.

3 Bake the cupcakes in the preheated oven for 20 minutes, or until risen and golden brown. While the cupcakes are baking, mix the topping ingredients together in a bowl.

4 Remove the cupcakes from the oven and let stand for 2 minutes, then spread some of the topping over each cupcake. Let cool in the pan—the topping will turn crisp on cooling.

pineapple
tropical cupcakes

MAKES 12

2 slices of canned pineapple in natural juice, plus 1 tbsp juice

6 tbsp butter, softened

scant ½ cup superfine sugar

1 extra large egg, lightly beaten

½ cup cup self-rising flour

frosting

2 tbsp butter, softened

scant ½ cup cream cheese

grated rind of 1 lemon or lime

scant 1 cup confectioners' sugar

1 tsp lemon juice or lime juice

1 Preheat the oven to 350°F/180°C. Put 12 paper liners in a muffin pan or put 12 double-layer paper liners on a baking sheet.

2 Finely chop the pineapple slices. Put the butter and sugar in a bowl and beat together until light and fluffy. Gradually beat in the egg. Add the flour and, using a large metal spoon, fold into the mixture. Fold in the chopped pineapple and the pineapple juice. Spoon the batter into the paper liners. Bake the cupcakes in the preheated oven for 20 minutes, or until well risen and golden brown. Transfer to a wire rack and let cool.

3 To make the frosting, put the butter and cream cheese in a large bowl and, using an electric mixer, beat together until smooth. Add the rind from the lemon. Sift the confectioners' sugar into the mixture, then beat together until well mixed. Gradually beat in the juice from the lemon, adding enough to form a spreading consistency. When the cupcakes are cold, spread the frosting on top of each cake, or fill a pastry bag fitted with a large star tip and pipe the frosting on top. Store the cupcakes in the refrigerator until ready to serve.

Step 2

Step 2

Step 2

mango & passion fruit cupcakes

MAKES 18

½ cup butter, softened

generous ½ cup superfine sugar

1 tsp finely grated orange rind

2 eggs, lightly beaten

generous ¾ cup self-rising flour

⅓ cup finely chopped dried mango

1 tbsp orange juice

icing

1¾ cups confectioners' sugar

seeds and pulp from 1 passion fruit

2 tbsp orange juice

1 Preheat the oven to 375°F/190°C. Put 18 paper liners in 2 muffin pans or put 18 double-layer paper liners on 2 baking sheets.

2 Put the butter, sugar, and orange rind in a mixing bowl and beat together until light and fluffy. Gradually beat in the eggs. Sift in the flour and, using a metal spoon, fold into the mixture with the chopped mango and orange juice. Spoon the batter into the paper liners.

3 Bake the cupcakes in the preheated oven for 20 minutes, or until golden brown and firm to the touch. Transfer to a wire rack and let cool.

4 To make the icing, sift the confectioners' sugar into a bowl and add the passion fruit seeds and pulp and 1 tablespoon of the orange juice. Mix to a smooth icing, adding the rest of the juice, if necessary. Spoon the icing over the cupcakes. Let set.

iced blueberry cupcakes

MAKES 30

1½ cups all-purpose flour

1 tbsp baking powder

¾ cup unsalted butter, softened

generous ¾ cup superfine sugar

3 eggs, beaten

1 tsp vanilla extract

finely grated rind of ½ orange

1⅓ cups fresh blueberries

icing

3 tbsp sour cream

1⅓ cups confectioners' sugar, sifted

1 Preheat the oven to 375°F/190°C. Put 30 paper liners into shallow muffin pans or put 30 double-layer liners onto baking sheets.

2 Sift the flour and baking powder into a large bowl and add the butter, superfine sugar, eggs, and vanilla extract. Beat well until the mixture is smooth. Add the orange rind and scant 1 cup of the blueberries.

3 Divide the batter among the paper liners. Bake in the preheated oven for 15–20 minutes, or until risen, firm, and golden brown. Transfer the cupcakes to a wire rack and let cool.

4 For the icing, stir the sour cream into the confectioners' sugar and mix well until smooth. Spoon a little on top of each cupcake and top with the remaining blueberries. Let set.

buttermilk cupcakes

MAKES 6

scant ⅔ cup butter, softened, plus extra for greasing

¾ cup superfine sugar

2 eggs, lightly beaten

4 tbsp buttermilk

1¼ cups self-rising flour

¾ cup blueberries

confectioners' sugar, for dusting

1 Preheat the oven to 375°F/190°C. Grease six 1-cup ovenproof dishes (such as ramekins) with butter.

2 Put the butter and sugar in a bowl and beat together until light and fluffy. Gradually beat in the eggs. Stir in the buttermilk. Sift in the flour and, using a metal spoon, fold into the mixture. Gently fold in half of the blueberries. Spoon the batter into the dishes. Scatter over the rest of the blueberries.

3 Put the dishes on a baking sheet and bake in the preheated oven for 25 minutes, until the cakes have risen and are firm to the touch. Serve warm or cold, dusted with sifted confectioners' sugar.

shredded orange cupcakes

MAKES 12

6 tbsp butter, softened

scant ½ cup superfine sugar

1 extra large egg, lightly beaten

generous ½ cup self-rising flour

generous ¼ cup ground almonds

grated rind and juice of 1 small orange

topping

grated rind and juice of 1 small orange

generous ¼ cup superfine sugar

2 tbsp toasted slivered almonds

1 Preheat the oven to 350°F/180°C. Put 12 paper liners in a muffin pan or put 12 double-layer paper liners on a baking sheet.

2 Put the butter and sugar in a bowl and beat together until light and fluffy. Gradually beat in the egg. Add the flour, ground almonds, and orange rind and, using a large metal spoon, fold into the mixture. Fold in the orange juice. Spoon the batter into the paper liners.

3 Bake the cupcakes in the preheated oven for 20–25 minutes, or until well risen and golden brown.

4 Meanwhile, make the topping. Put the orange rind and juice and the sugar in a pan and heat gently, stirring, until the sugar has dissolved, then let simmer for 5 minutes.

5 When the cupcakes have cooked, prick them all over with a skewer. Spoon the warm syrup and the rind over each cupcake, then sprinkle the slivered almonds on top. Transfer to a wire rack and let cool.

Step 2

Step 2

Step 5

carrot & orange cupcakes

MAKES 12

½ cup butter, softened

⅔ cup light brown sugar

juice and finely grated rind of 1 small orange

2 extra large eggs, lightly beaten

1⅔ cups grated carrots

¼ cup coarsely chopped walnut pieces

scant 1 cup all-purpose flour

1 tsp ground pumpkin pie spice

1½ tsp baking powder

frosting

1¼ cups mascarpone cheese

¼ cups confectioners' sugar

grated rind of 1 large orange

1 Preheat the oven to 350°F/180°C. Put 12 muffin paper liners in a muffin pan or put 12 double-layer paper liners on a baking sheet.

2 Put the butter, sugar, and orange rind in a bowl and beat together until light and fluffy. Gradually add the eggs, beating well after each addition. Squeeze any excess liquid from the carrots and add to the mixture with the walnuts and orange juice. Stir into the mixture until well mixed. Sift the flour, pumpkin pie spice, and baking powder into the bowl and then, using a metal spoon, fold into the mixture. Spoon the batter into the paper liners.

3 Bake the cupcakes in the preheated oven for 25 minutes, or until well risen, firm to the touch, and golden brown. Transfer to a wire rack and let cool.

4 To make the frosting, put the mascarpone cheese, confectioners' sugar, and orange rind in a large bowl and beat together until well mixed.

5 When the cupcakes are cold, spread the frosting on top of each cupcake, swirling it with a round-bladed knife. Store the cupcakes in the refrigerator until ready to serve.

raspberry almond cupcakes

MAKES 14

½ cup butter, softened

scant ½ cup superfine sugar

½ tsp almond extract

2 eggs, lightly beaten

scant ⅔ cup self-rising flour

scant ⅔ cup ground almonds

⅔ cup fresh raspberries

2 tbsp slivered almonds

confectioners' sugar, for dusting

1 Preheat the oven to 350°F/180°C. Put 14 paper liners in 2 muffin pans or put 14 double-layer paper liners on a baking sheet.

2 Put the butter, sugar, and almond extract in a bowl and beat together until light and fluffy. Gradually beat in the eggs. Sift in the flour and, using a metal spoon, fold into the mixture with the ground almonds. Gently fold in the raspberries. Spoon the batter into the paper liners. Scatter the slivered almonds over the top.

3 Bake the cupcakes in the preheated oven for 25–30 minutes, or until golden brown and firm to the touch. Transfer to a wire rack and let cool. Dust with confectioners' sugar.

blackberry crumble cupcakes

MAKES 6

generous ¾ cup self-rising flour

½ tsp baking powder

½ cup butter, softened, plus extra for greasing

generous ½ cup superfine sugar

2 eggs

1¼ cups blackberries

whipped cream, to serve

topping

scant ⅔ cup self-rising flour

¼ cup raw brown sugar

4 tbsp butter, chilled and diced

1 Preheat the oven to 375°F/190°C. Grease six 1-cup ovenproof dishes (such as ramekins) with butter.

2 To make the topping, mix the flour and sugar in a bowl. Add the butter and rub in until the mixture resembles course breadcrumbs.

3 To make the cake, sift the flour and baking powder into a bowl. Add the butter, superfine sugar, and eggs and, using an electric mixer, beat together until smooth. Spoon the batter into the dishes and level the surface. Top with the blackberries. Spoon the crumble mixture over the blackberries.

4 Put the dishes on a baking sheet and bake in the preheated oven for 25–30 minutes, until the crumble topping is golden brown. Serve warm with whipped cream.

hummingbird cupcakes

MAKES 12

generous 1¼ cups all- purpose flour

¾ tsp baking soda

1 tsp ground cinnamon

generous ½ cup light brown sugar

2 eggs, beaten

scant ½ cup sunflower oil

⅓ cup mashed ripe banana

2 canned pineapple rings, drained and finely chopped

¼ cup finely chopped pecans, plus extra sliced pecans to decorate

frosting

⅔ cup cream cheese

5 tbsp unsalted butter, softened

1 tsp vanilla extract

2½ cups confectioners' sugar, sifted

1 Preheat the oven to 350°F/180°C. Put 12 paper liners in a muffin pan or put 12 double-layer liners on a large baking sheet.

2 Sift the flour, baking soda, and cinnamon into a bowl and stir in the sugar. Add the eggs, oil, banana, pineapple, and chopped pecans and mix thoroughly. Spoon the batter into the paper liners.

3 Bake the cupcakes for 15–20 minutes, until risen, golden, and firm to the touch. Transfer to a wire rack and let cool.

4 To make the frosting, put the cream cheese, butter, and vanilla extract in a bowl and blend together with a spatula. Beat in the confectioners' sugar until smooth and creamy. Pipe or swirl the frosting on the top of the cupcakes. Decorate with sliced pecans.

Step 2

Step 2

Step 4

cranberry cupcakes

MAKES 14

5½ tbsp butter, softened

½ cup superfine sugar

1 extra large egg

2 tbsp milk

¾ cup self-rising flour

1 tsp baking powder

scant ¾ cup frozen cranberries

1 Preheat the oven to 350°F/180°C. Put 14 paper liners in 2 muffin pans or put 14 double-layer paper liners on a baking sheet.

2 Put the butter and sugar in a bowl and beat together until light and fluffy. Gradually beat in the egg, then stir in the milk. Sift in the flour and baking powder and, using a large metal spoon, fold them into the mixture. Gently fold in the frozen cranberries. Spoon the batter into the paper liners.

3 Bake the cupcakes in the preheated oven for 15–20 minutes, or until well risen and golden brown. Transfer to a wire rack and let cool.

whole wheat apricot cupcakes

MAKES 14

½ cup butter, softened

scant ½ cup brown sugar

2 tbsp honey

2 eggs, lightly beaten

generous ⅔ cup whole wheat all-purpose flour

1½ tsp baking powder

1 tsp ground allspice

½ cup chopped plumped dried apricots

2 tbsp apricot jelly, warmed, or apricot conserve, warmed and strained

slices of plumped dried apricots, to decorate

1 Preheat the oven to 375°F/190°C. Put 14 paper liners in 2 muffin pans or put 14 double-layer paper liners on a baking sheet.

2 Put the butter, sugar, and honey in a bowl and beat together until light and fluffy. Gradually add the eggs, beating well after each addition. Sift in the flour, baking powder, and allspice (tipping any bran left in the sifter into the bowl) and, using a metal spoon, fold them into the mixture with the chopped apricots. Spoon the batter into the paper liners.

3 Bake the cupcakes in the preheated oven for 15–20 minutes, or until risen, golden brown, and firm to the touch. Transfer and let a wire rack to cool.

4 When the cupcakes are cold, brush the apricot jelly over the top of each cupcake and decorate each with a slice of apricot.

spiced plum cupcakes

MAKES 4

4 tbsp butter, softened, plus extra for greasing

¼ cup superfine sugar

1 extra large egg, lightly beaten

scant ½ cup whole wheat flour

½ tsp baking powder

1 tsp ground allspice

generous ¼ cup coarsely ground blanched hazelnuts

2 small plums, halved, pitted, and sliced

Greek yogurt, to serve

1 Preheat the oven to 350°F/180°C. Grease four ⅔-cup ovenproof dishes (such as ramekins) with butter.

2 Put the butter and sugar in a bowl and beat together until light and fluffy. Gradually beat in the egg. Sift in the flour, baking powder, and allspice (tipping any bran left in the sieve into the bowl) and, using a metal spoon, fold into the mixture with the ground hazelnuts. Spoon the batter into the dishes. Arrange the sliced plums on top of the batter.

3 Put the dishes on a baking sheet and bake in the preheated oven for 25 minutes, or until risen and firm to the touch. Serve warm or cold with Greek yogurt.

apple streusel cupcakes

MAKES 14

½ **tsp baking soda**

1¼ **cups tart applesauce**

4 **tbsp butter, softened**

scant ½ **cup raw brown sugar**

1 **extra large egg, lightly beaten**

scant 1¼ **cups self-rising flour**

½ **tsp ground cinnamon**

½ **tsp freshly ground nutmeg**

topping

generous ⅓ **cup all-purpose flour**

¼ **cup raw brown sugar**

¼ **tsp ground cinnamon**

¼ **tsp freshly grated nutmeg**

2½ **tbsp butter**

1 Preheat the oven to 350°F/180°C. Put 14 paper liners in 2 muffin pans or put 14 double-layer paper liners on a baking sheet.

2 To make the topping, put the flour, sugar, cinnamon, and nutmeg in a bowl. Cut the butter into small pieces, then rub into the mixture.

3 To make the cupcakes, add the baking soda to the applesauce and stir until dissolved. Put the butter and sugar in a bowl and beat together until light and fluffy. Gradually beat in the egg. Sift in the flour, cinnamon, and nutmeg and, using a large metal spoon, fold into the mixture, alternating with the applesauce.

4 Spoon the batter into the paper liners. Sprinkle the topping over each cupcake to cover the tops and press down gently. Bake the cupcakes in the preheated oven for 20 minutes, or until well risen and golden brown. Let the cakes cool for 2–3 minutes before serving warm or transfer to a wire rack and let cool.

Step 2

Step 3

Step 3

coconut cherry cupcakes

MAKES 12

½ cup butter, softened

generous ½ cup superfine sugar

2 tbsp milk

2 eggs, lightly beaten

generous ½ cup self-rising flour

½ tsp baking powder

⅔ cup dry flaked unsweetened coconut

½ cup quartered candied cherries

12 whole candied, maraschino, or fresh cherries, to decorate

frosting

4 tbsp butter, softened

1 cup confectioners' sugar

1 tbsp milk

1 Preheat the oven to 350°F/180°C. Put 12 paper liners in a muffin pan or put 12 double-layer paper liners on a baking sheet.

2 Put the butter and sugar in a bowl and beat together until light and fluffy. Stir in the milk. Gradually add the eggs, beating well after each addition. Sift in the flour and baking powder and fold them in with the coconut. Gently fold in most of the quartered cherries. Spoon the batter into the paper liners and sprinkle the remaining quartered cherries on top.

3 Bake the cupcakes in the preheated oven for 20–25 minutes, or until well risen, golden brown, and firm to the touch. Transfer to a wire rack and let cool.

4 To make the frosting, put the butter in a bowl and beat until fluffy. Sift in the confectioners' sugar and beat together until well mixed, gradually beating in the milk.

5 To decorate the cupcakes, using a pastry bag fitted with a large star tip, pipe the buttercream on top of each cupcake, then add a candied, maraschino, or fresh cherry to decorate.

almond & apricot spice cupcakes

MAKES 30

1½ **cups all-purpose flour**

1 tbsp baking powder

1 tsp ground allspice

¾ **cup unsalted butter, softened**

generous ¾ **cup superfine sugar**

3 eggs, beaten

1 tsp almond extract

2 tbsp milk

⅓ **cup finely chopped plumped dried apricots**

⅓ **cup ground almonds**

generous ⅔ **cup dulce de leche**

¼ **cup toasted slivered almonds**

1 Preheat the oven to 375°F/190°C. Put 30 paper liners into shallow muffin pans or put 30 double-layer liners onto baking sheets.

2 Sift the flour, baking powder, and allspice into a large bowl and add the butter, sugar, eggs, and almond extract. Beat well until the mixture is smooth, then stir in the milk, apricots, and ground almonds.

3 Divide the batter among the paper liners. Bake in the preheated oven for 15–20 minutes, or until risen, firm, and golden brown. Transfer the cupcakes to a wire rack and let cool.

4 Spoon about a teaspoonful of the dulce de leche on top of each cupcake, then top with the slivered almonds.

pistachio cupcakes

MAKES 16

generous ¾ cup shelled, unsalted pistachio nuts

½ cup butter, softened

¾ cup superfine sugar

1 cup self-rising flour

2 eggs, lightly beaten

4 tbsp Greek yogurt

frosting

½ cup butter, softened

2 tbsp sweetened lime juice

few drops green food coloring (optional)

1¾ cups confectioners' sugar

1 tbsp chopped pistachio nuts

1 Preheat the oven to 350°F/180°C. Put 16 paper liners in 2 muffin pans or put 16 double-layer paper liners on a baking sheet.

2 Put the pistachio nuts in a food processor or blender and process for a few seconds until finely ground. Add the butter, sugar, flour, eggs, and yogurt and process until evenly mixed. Spoon the batter into the paper liners.

3 Bake the cupcakes in the preheated oven for 20–25 minutes, or until golden brown and firm to the touch. Transfer to a wire rack and let cool.

4 To make the frosting, put the butter, lime juice, and food coloring (if using) in a bowl and beat until fluffy. Sift in the confectioners' sugar and beat until smooth. Swirl the frosting over each cupcake and sprinkle with the chopped pistachio nuts.

banana & pecan cupcakes

MAKES 24

1½ cups all-purpose flour

1¼ tsp baking powder

¼ tsp baking soda

2 ripe bananas

½ cup butter, softened

generous ½ cup superfine sugar

½ tsp vanilla extract

2 eggs, lightly beaten

4 tbsp sour cream

½ cup coarsely chopped pecans

topping

½ cup butter, softened

1 cup confectioners' sugar

¼ cup chopped pecans

1 Preheat the oven to 375°F/190°C. Put 24 paper liners in 2 muffin pans or put 24 double-layer paper liners on 2 baking sheets.

2 Sift together the flour, baking powder, and baking soda. Peel the bananas, put them in a bowl, and mash with a fork.

3 Put the butter, sugar, and vanilla in a bowl and beat together until light and fluffy. Gradually add the eggs, beating well after each addition. Stir in the mashed bananas and sour cream. Using a metal spoon, fold in the sifted flour mixture and chopped nuts, then spoon the batter into the paper liners.

4 Bake the cupcakes in the preheated oven for 20 minutes, or until well risen and golden brown. Transfer to a wire rack and let cool.

5 For the topping, put the butter in a bowl and beat until fluffy. Sift in the confectioners' sugar and mix together well. Spread the frosting on top of each cupcake and sprinkle with the chopped pecans before serving.

Step 2

Step 3

Step 3

macadamia &
maple cupcakes

MAKES 10

6 tbsp butter, softened

¼ cup brown sugar

2 tbsp maple syrup

1 extra large egg, lightly beaten

⅔ cup self-rising flour

½ cup chopped macadamia nuts

1 tbsp milk

frosting

2 tbsp butter, softened

2 tbsp maple syrup

¾ cup confectioners' sugar, sifted

⅓ cup cream cheese

2 tbsp chopped macadamia nuts, lightly toasted

1 Preheat the oven to 375°F/190°C. Put 10 paper liners in a muffin pan or put 10 double-layer paper liners on a baking sheet.

2 Put the butter, sugar, and maple syrup in a bowl and beat together until light and fluffy. Gradually beat in the egg. Sift in the flour and, using a metal spoon, fold into the mixture with the nuts and milk. Spoon the batter into the paper liners.

3 Bake the cupcakes in the preheated oven for 20 minutes, or until golden brown and firm to the touch. Transfer to a wire rack and let cool.

4 To make the frosting, beat the butter and maple syrup together until smooth. Sift in the confectioners' sugar and beat in thoroughly. Gently beat in the cream cheese. Swirl the frosting on the top of each cake and sprinkle over the toasted nuts.

pure indulgence almond cupcakes

MAKES 12

7 tbsp butter, softened

½ cup superfine sugar

2 eggs, lightly beaten

¼ tsp almond extract

4 tbsp light cream

1¼ cups all-purpose flour

1½ tsp baking powder

¾ cup ground almonds

topping

½ cup butter, softened

2 cups confectioners' sugar

few drops of almond extract

¼ cup toasted slivered almonds

1 Preheat the oven to 350°F/180°C. Put 12 paper liners in a muffin pan or put 12 double-layer paper liners on a baking sheet.

2 Place the butter and sugar in a large bowl and beat together until light and fluffy. Gradually beat in the eggs, then add the almond extract and cream. Sift in the flour and baking powder and fold into the batter, then fold in the ground almonds. Spoon the batter into the paper liners.

3 Bake in the preheated oven for 25 minutes, or until golden brown and firm to the touch. Let the cupcakes cool in the pan for 10 minutes, then transfer to a wire rack and let cool completely.

4 To make the topping, place the butter in a large bowl and beat until creamy. Sift in the confectioners' sugar. Add the almond extract and beat until smooth. Spread the topping on top of each cake, using a knife to form the topping into swirls. Sprinkle the almonds over the top.

sticky date cupcakes

MAKES 6

½ **cup chopped, pitted dried dates**

½ **tsp baking soda**

⅓ **cup water**

6 **tbsp butter, softened, plus extra for greasing**

scant ½ **cup dark brown sugar**

1 **tsp vanilla extract**

2 **eggs, lightly beaten**

generous ½ **cup self-rising flour**

whipped cream, to serve

caramel sauce

scant ½ **cup dark brown sugar**

4 **tbsp butter**

4 **tbsp heavy cream**

1 Put the dates, baking soda, and water in a small saucepan and bring to a boil. Remove from the heat and set aside to cool.

2 Preheat the oven to 350°F/180°C. Grease six ¾-cup ovenproof dishes (such as ramekins) with butter.

3 Put the butter, sugar, and vanilla extract in a bowl and beat together until light and fluffy. Gradually beat in the eggs. Sift in the flour and, using a metal spoon, fold into the mixture followed by the date mixture. Spoon the batter into the dishes.

4 Put the dishes on a baking sheet and bake in the preheated oven for 20–25 minutes, or until risen and firm to the touch.

5 To make the caramel sauce, put all the ingredients in a small saucepan and heat until the butter has melted. Simmer for 5 minutes, stirring occasionally. Using a skewer, prick a few holes in each warm cupcake and drizzle over some of the sauce. Serve the cupcakes with the rest of the caramel sauce and whipped cream.

moist walnut cupcakes

MAKES 12

¾ **cup walnuts**

4 tbsp butter, softened

½ **cup superfine sugar**

grated rind of ½ **lemon**

½ **cup self-rising flour**

2 eggs

12 walnut halves, to decorate

frosting

4 tbsp butter, softened

¾ **cup confectioners' sugar**

grated rind of ½ **lemon**

1 tsp lemon juice

1 Preheat the oven to 375°F/190°C. Put 12 paper liners in a muffin pan or put 12 double-layer paper liners on a baking sheet.

2 Put the walnuts in a food processor and, using a pulsating action, blend until finely ground, being careful not to overgrind, which will turn them to oil. Add the butter, cut into small pieces, along with the sugar, lemon rind, flour, and eggs, then blend until evenly mixed. Spoon the batter into the paper liners.

3 Bake the cupcakes in the preheated oven for 20 minutes, or until well risen and golden brown. Transfer to a wire rack and let cool.

4 To make the frosting, put the butter in a bowl and beat until fluffy. Sift in the confectioners' sugar, add the lemon rind and juice, and mix well together.

5 When the cupcakes are cold, spread the frosting on top of each cupcake and top with a walnut half to decorate.

VARIATION

Replace the walnuts with pecans and the lemon rind and juice with orange rind and juice to make moist pecan cupcakes.

4

Superbly
Special

coffee fudge cupcakes

MAKES 28

1½ cups all-purpose flour

1 tbsp baking powder

¾ cup unsalted butter, softened

generous ¾ cup superfine sugar

3 eggs, beaten

1 tsp coffee extract

2 tbsp milk

chocolate-covered coffee beans, to decorate

frosting

4 tbsp unsalted butter

generous ½ cup light brown sugar

2 tbsp light cream or milk

½ tsp coffee extract

3½ cups confectioners' sugar, sifted

1 Preheat the oven to 375°F/190°C. Put 28 paper liners into shallow muffin pans or put 28 double-layer liners onto baking sheets.

2 Sift the flour and baking powder into a large bowl and add the butter, superfine sugar, eggs, and coffee extract. Beat well until the mixture is smooth, then beat in the milk.

3 Divide the batter among the paper liners. Bake in the preheated oven for 15–20 minutes, or until risen, firm, and golden brown. Transfer the cupcakes to a wire rack and let cool.

4 For the frosting, put the butter, brown sugar, cream, and coffee extract into a pan over medium heat and stir until smooth. Bring to a boil and boil for 2 minutes, stirring. Remove from the heat and beat in the confectioners' sugar.

5 Stir until smooth and thick, then spoon into a pastry bag fitted with a large star tip. Pipe a swirl of frosting on top of each cupcake and top with a coffee bean.

marzipan flower cupcakes

MAKES 12

generous ¾ cup self-rising flour

½ tsp baking powder

½ cup soft margarine

generous ½ cup superfine sugar

2 eggs, lightly beaten

few drops almond extract

topping

7 oz/200 g natural marzipan

confectioners' sugar, for dusting

2 tbsp apricot jelly

1 Preheat the oven to 350°F/180°C. Put 12 paper liners in a muffin pan or put 12 double-layer paper liners on a baking sheet.

2 Sift the flour and baking powder into a bowl. Add the margarine, sugar, eggs, and almond extract and, using an electric mixer, beat together until smooth. Spoon the batter into the paper liners.

3 Bake the cupcakes in the preheated oven for 20 minutes, or until golden brown and firm to the touch. Transfer to a wire rack and let cool.

4 For the topping, roll out the marzipan on a surface dusted lightly with confectioners' sugar. Using a 1¼-inch/3-cm round cutter, stamp out 60 circles, reusing the marzipan as necessary. Spread a little apricot jelly over the top of each cupcake. Pinch the marzipan circles on one side to create petal shapes and arrange five petals on top of each cupcake. Roll small balls of the remaining marzipan for the flower centers and place in the middle of the cupcakes.

apple pie cupcakes

MAKES 12

3½ **tbsp butter, softened**

⅓ **cup raw brown sugar**

1 **egg, lightly beaten**

generous 1 **cup all-purpose flour**

1½ **tsp baking powder**

½ **tsp apple pie spice**

1 **large baking apple, peeled, cored, and finely chopped**

1 **tbsp orange juice**

topping

5 **tbsp all-purpose flour**

½ **tsp apple pie spice**

2 **tbsp butter**

¼ **cup superfine sugar**

1 Preheat the oven to 350°F/180°C. Put 12 paper liners in a muffin pan or put 12 double-layer paper liners on a baking sheet.

2 To make the topping, place the flour, apple pie spice, butter, and sugar in a large bowl and rub in with your fingertips until the mixture resembles fine breadcrumbs. Set aside.

3 To make the cupcakes, place the butter and sugar in a large bowl and beat together until light and fluffy, then gradually beat in the egg. Sift in the flour, baking powder, and apple pie spice and fold into the mixture, then fold in the chopped apple and orange juice. Spoon the batter into the paper liners. Add the topping to cover the top of each cupcake and press down gently.

4 Bake in the preheated oven for 30 minutes, or until golden brown. Let the cupcakes cool in the pan for 2–3 minutes and serve warm, or let cool for 10 minutes and then transfer to a wire rack to cool completely.

birthday party cupcakes

MAKES 24

1 cup soft margarine

generous 1⅛ cups superfine sugar

4 eggs

scant 1⅝ cups self-rising flour

topping

¾ cup butter, softened

3 cups confectioners' sugar

a variety of small candies and chocolates, sugar-coated chocolates, dried fruits, edible sugar flower shapes, cake decorating sprinkles, silver dragées (cake decoration balls), and sugar strands

24 birthday cake candles (optional)

1 Preheat the oven to 350°F/180°C. Put 24 paper liners in 2 muffin pans or put 24 double-layer paper liners on 2 baking sheets.

2 Put the margarine, sugar, eggs, and flour in a large bowl and, using an electric mixer, beat together until just smooth. Spoon the batter into the paper liners.

3 Bake the cupcakes in the preheated oven for 15–20 minutes, or until well risen, golden brown, and firm to the touch. Transfer to a wire rack and let cool.

4 To make the topping, put the butter in a bowl and beat until fluffy. Sift in the confectioners' sugar and beat together until smooth and creamy.

5 When the cupcakes are cold pipe the frosting on top of each cupcake, then decorate to your choice and, if desired, place a candle in the top of each.

Step 2

Step 4

Step 5

christmas cupcakes

MAKES 16

generous ½ cup butter, softened

1 cup superfine sugar

4–6 drops almond extract

4 eggs, lightly beaten

generous 1 cup self-rising flour

1¾ cups ground almonds

topping

1 lb/450 g white ready-to-use fondant

2 oz/55 g green ready-to-use fondant

1 oz/25 g red ready-to-use fondant

confectioners' sugar, for dusting

1 Preheat the oven to 350°F/180°C. Put 16 paper liners in 2 muffin pans or put 18 double-layer paper liners on a large baking sheet.

2 Put the butter, sugar, and almond extract in a bowl and beat together until light and fluffy. Gradually add the eggs, beating well after each addition. Add the flour and, using a large metal spoon, fold it into the mixture, then fold in the ground almonds. Spoon the batter into the paper liners to fill them halfway.

3 Bake the cakes in the preheated oven for 20 minutes, or until well risen, golden brown, and firm to the touch. Transfer to a wire rack and let cool.

4 When the cakes are cold, knead the white fondant until pliable, then roll out on a surface lightly dusted with confectioners' sugar. Using a 2¾-inch/7-cm plain round cutter, cut out 16 circles, rerolling the fondant as necessary. Place a circle on top of each cupcake.

5 Roll out the green fondant on a surface lightly dusted with confectioners' sugar. Using the palm of your hand, rub confectioners' sugar into the fondant to prevent it from spotting. Using a holly leaf-shaped cutter, cut out 32 leaves, rerolling the fondant as necessary. Brush each leaf with a little cooled boiled water and place 2 leaves on top of each cake. Roll the red fondant between the palms of your hands to form 48 berries and place in the center of the leaves.

festive cupcakes

MAKES 14

⅔ cup mixed dried fruit

1 tsp finely grated orange rind

2 tbsp brandy or orange juice

6 tbsp butter, softened

scant ½ cup brown sugar

1 extra large egg, lightly beaten

generous ¾ cup self-rising flour

1 tsp ground allspice

1 tbsp silver dragées (cake decoration balls), to decorate

icing

¾ cup confectioners' sugar

2 tbsp orange juice

1 Put the mixed fruit, orange rind, and brandy or orange juice in a small bowl, cover, and let soak for 1 hour.

2 Preheat the oven to 375°F/190°C. Put 14 paper liners in 2 muffin pans or put 14 double-layer paper liners on a baking sheet.

3 Put the butter and sugar in a mixing bowl and beat together until light and fluffy. Gradually beat in the egg. Sift in the flour and allspice and, using a metal spoon, fold them into the mixture followed by the soaked fruit. Spoon the batter into the paper liners.

4 Bake the cupcakes in the preheated oven for 15–20 minutes, or until golden brown and firm to the touch. Transfer to a wire rack and let cool.

5 To make the icing, sift the confectioners' sugar into a bowl and gradually mix in enough orange juice until the mixture is smooth and thick enough to coat the back of a wooden spoon. Using a teaspoon, drizzle the icing in a zigzag pattern over the cupcakes. Decorate with the silver dragées. Let set.

valentine heart cupcakes

MAKES 6

scant ½ cup butter, softened

generous ⅜ cup superfine sugar

½ tsp vanilla extract

2 eggs, lightly beaten

½ cup all-purpose flour

1 tbsp unsweetened cocoa

1 tsp baking powder

marzipan hearts

1¼ oz/35 g marzipan

red food coloring (liquid or paste)

confectioners' sugar, for dusting

topping

4 tbsp butter, softened

1 cup confectioners' sugar

1 oz/25 g semisweet chocolate, melted

6 edible candy flowers, to decorate

1 To make the hearts, knead the marzipan until pliable, then add a few drops of red coloring and knead until evenly colored red. Roll out the marzipan to a thickness of ¼ inch/5 mm on a surface dusted with confectioners' sugar. Using a small heart-shaped cutter, cut out 6 hearts. Put these on a baking sheet lined with wax paper and dusted with confectioners' sugar. Let dry for 3–4 hours.

2 To make the cupcakes, preheat the oven to 350°F/180°C. Put 6 muffin paper liners in a muffin pan or put 6 double-layer paper liners on a baking sheet.

3 Put the butter, sugar, and vanilla extract in a bowl and beat together until light and fluffy. Gradually add the eggs, beating well after each addition. Sift in the flour, cocoa, and baking powder and, using a large metal spoon, fold into the mixture. Spoon the batter into the paper liners.

4 Bake the cupcakes in the preheated oven for 20–25 minutes, or until well risen and firm to the touch. Transfer to a wire rack and let cool.

5 For the frosting, put the butter in a large bowl and beat until fluffy. Sift in the confectioners' sugar and beat together until smooth. Add the melted chocolate and beat together until well mixed. When the cakes are cold, spread the frosting on top of each cake, decorate with edible candy flowers, and add the marzipan hearts.

easter cupcakes

MAKES 12

½ cup butter, softened

generous ½ cup superfine sugar

2 eggs, lightly beaten

generous ½ cup self-rising flour

generous ¼ cup unsweetened cocoa

topping

6 tbsp butter, softened

1½ cups confectioners' sugar

1 tbsp milk

2–3 drops of vanilla extract

two 4¾-oz/130-g packages mini chocolate candy shell eggs

1 Preheat the oven to 350°F/180°C. Put 12 paper liners in a muffin pan or put 12 double-layer paper liners on a baking sheet.

2 Put the butter and sugar in a bowl and beat together until light and fluffy. Gradually add the eggs, beating well after each addition. Sift in the flour and cocoa and, using a large metal spoon, fold into the mixture. Spoon the batter into the paper liners.

3 Bake the cupcakes in the preheated oven for 15–20 minutes, or until well risen and firm to the touch. Transfer to a wire rack and let cool.

4 For the topping, put the butter in a bowl and beat until fluffy. Sift in the confectioners' sugar and beat together until well mixed, adding the milk and vanilla extract.

5 When the cupcakes are cold, put the frosting in a pastry bag fitted with a large star tip, and pipe a circle around the edge of each cupcake. Decorate with chocolate eggs.

Step 2

Step 4

Step 5

halloween cupcakes

MAKES 12

½ **cup soft margarine**

generous ½ **cup superfine sugar**

2 **eggs**

generous ¾ **cup self-rising flour**

topping

7 oz/200 g orange **ready-to-use fondant**

confectioners' sugar, **for dusting**

2 oz/55 g black ready-**to-use fondant**

black cake-writing frosting

yellow writing icing

1 Preheat the oven to 350°F/180°C. Put 12 paper liners in a muffin pan or put 12 double-layer paper liners on a baking sheet.

2 Put the margarine, sugar, eggs, and flour in a bowl and, using an electric mixer, beat together until smooth. Spoon the batter into the liners.

3 Bake the cupcakes in the preheated oven for 15–20 minutes, or until well risen, golden brown, and firm to the touch. Transfer to a wire rack and let cool.

4 When the cupcakes are cold, knead the orange fondant until pliable, then roll out on a surface dusted with confectioners' sugar. Using the palm of your hand, lightly rub confectioners' sugar into the fondant to prevent it from spotting. Using a 2¼-inch/5.5-cm plain round cutter, cut out 12 circles, rerolling the fondant as necessary. Place a circle on top of each cupcake.

5 Roll out the black fondant on a surface lightly dusted with confectioners' sugar. Using the palm of your hand, lightly rub confectioners' sugar into the fondant to prevent it from spotting. Using a 1¼-inch/3-cm plain round cutter, cut out 12 circles and place them on the center of the cupcakes. Using black writing icing, pipe 8 legs onto each spider and using yellow writing icing, draw 2 eyes and a mouth.

baby shower cupcakes

1¾ cups butter, softened

2 cups superfine sugar

finely grated rind of 2 lemons

4 eggs, lightly beaten

generous 2¾ cups self-rising flour

topping

3 cups confectioners' sugar

red or blue food coloring (liquid or paste)

24 sugared almonds

1 Preheat the oven to 350°F/180°C. Put 24 paper liners in 2 muffin pans or put 24 double-layer paper liners on a large baking sheet.

2 Put the butter, sugar, and lemon rind in a bowl and beat together until light and fluffy. Gradually add the eggs, beating well after each addition. Add the flour and, using a large metal spoon, fold into the mixture. Spoon the batter into the paper liners to fill them halfway.

3 Bake the cupcakes in the preheated oven for 20–25 minutes, or until well risen, golden brown, and firm to the touch. Transfer to a wire rack and let cool.

4 When the cakes are cold, make the topping. Sift the confectioners' sugar into a bowl. Add 6–8 teaspoons of hot water and stir until the mixture is smooth and thick enough to coat the back of a wooden spoon. Dip a skewer into the red or blue food coloring, then stir it into the icing until it is evenly colored pink or pale blue.

5 Spoon the icing on top of each cupcake. Top each with a sugared almond and let set for about 30 minutes before serving.

gold star cupcakes

MAKES 12

6 tbsp butter, softened

scant ½ cup light brown sugar

1 extra large egg, beaten

scant ⅔ cup self-rising flour

½ tsp ground cinnamon

1 tbsp milk

gold stars

3 oz/ 85 g yellow ready-to-use fondant

confectioners' sugar, for dusting

edible gold dusting powder (optional)

icing

¾ cup confectioners' sugar

2–3 tsp lemon juice

1 Preheat the oven to 350°F/180°C. Put 12 paper liners in a muffin pan or put 12 double-layer paper liners on a baking sheet.

2 Put the butter and sugar in a mixing bowl and beat together until light and fluffy. Gradually beat in the egg. Sift in the flour and cinnamon and, using a metal spoon, fold them into the mixture with the milk. Spoon the batter into the paper liners.

3 Bake the cupcakes in the preheated oven for 20 minutes, or until golden brown and firm to the touch. Transfer to a wire rack and let cool.

4 To make the gold stars, roll the yellow fondant out on a surface lightly dusted with confectioners' sugar and, using a small star cutter, stamp out 12 stars. Brush each star with a little gold dusting powder, if using. Set aside on a sheet of parchment paper.

5 To make the icing, sift the confectioners' sugar into a bowl and stir in enough lemon juice to make a smooth and thick icing.

6 Spoon the icing on top of the cupcakes and top each with a gold star. Let set.

anniversary cupcakes

MAKES 24

1 cup butter, softened

generous 1 cup superfine sugar

1 tsp vanilla extract

4 extra large eggs, lightly beaten

generous 1½ cups self rising flour

5 tbsp milk

topping

¾ cup unsalted butter

3 cups confectioners' sugar

silver or gold dragées (cake decoration balls)

1 Preheat the oven to 350°F/180°C. Put 24 silver or gold foil cake liners in muffin pans, or arrange them on baking sheets.

2 Put the butter, sugar, and vanilla extract in a bowl and beat together until light and fluffy. Gradually add the eggs, beating well after each addition. Add the flour and, using a large metal spoon, fold into the mixture with the milk. Spoon the batter into the paper liners.

3 Bake the cupcakes in the preheated oven for 15–20 minutes, or until well risen and firm to the touch. Transfer to a wire rack and let cool.

4 For the topping, put the butter in a large bowl and beat until fluffy. Sift in the confectioners' sugar and beat together until well mixed. Put the topping in a pastry bag, fitted with a medium star-shaped tip.

5 When the cupcakes are cold, pipe the frosting over the top of each one. Sprinkle over the silver or gold dragées before serving.

Step 2

Step 2

Step 5

cherry cupcakes

MAKES 28

1½ cups all-purpose flour

⅓ cup chopped candied cherries

1 tbsp baking powder

1 tbsp cornstarch

¾ cup unsalted butter, softened

generous ¾ cup superfine sugar

3 eggs, beaten

1 tsp vanilla extract

14 candied cherries, halved, to decorate

frosting

generous 1 cup ricotta cheese

⅔ cup confectioners' sugar

½ tsp vanilla extract

1 Preheat the oven to 375°F/190°C. Put 28 paper liners into shallow muffin pans or put double-layer liners onto baking sheets.

2 Stir a tablespoon of the flour into the cherries. Sift the remaining flour with the baking powder and cornstarch into a large bowl and add the butter, superfine sugar, eggs, and vanilla extract. Beat well until the mixture is smooth, then stir in the cherries.

3 Divide the batter among the paper liners. Bake in the preheated oven for 15–20 minutes, or until risen, firm, and golden brown. Transfer the cupcakes to a wire rack and let cool.

4 For the frosting, combine the ricotta, confectioners' sugar, and vanilla extract, then spoon a little on top of each cupcake. Top each with half a candied cherry.

vanilla hazelnut yogurt cupcakes

MAKES 26

1½ cups all-purpose flour

2 tsp cornstarch

1 tbsp baking powder

¾ cup plain yogurt

generous ¾ cup superfine sugar

3 eggs, beaten

1 tsp vanilla extract

⅓ cup finely chopped hazelnuts

topping

scant 1 cup confectioners' sugar, sifted

3 tbsp plain yogurt

⅓ cup coarsely chopped hazelnuts

1 Preheat the oven to 375°F/190°C. Put 26 paper liners into shallow muffin pans or put 26 double-layer liners onto baking sheets.

2 Sift the flour, cornstarch, and baking powder into a large bowl and add the yogurt, sugar, eggs, and vanilla extract. Beat well until the mixture is smooth, then stir in the finely chopped hazelnuts.

3 Divide the batter among the paper liners. Bake in the preheated oven for 15–20 minutes, or until risen, firm, and golden brown. Transfer the cupcakes to a wire rack and let cool.

4 For the topping, combine the confectioners' sugar and yogurt until smooth, then drizzle the mixture over the cupcakes. Sprinkle with the coarsely chopped hazelnuts and let set.

orange saffron mini cupcakes

MAKES 90

2–3 tbsp orange juice

pinch of saffron threads

1½ cups all-purpose flour

1 tbsp baking powder

¾ cup unsalted butter, softened

generous ¾ cup superfine sugar

3 eggs, beaten

finely grated rind of 1 orange

1⅓ cups confectioners' sugar, sifted

fine strips of orange zest

1 Preheat the oven to 375°F/190°C. Arrange 90 mini paper liners on 2–3 baking sheets.

2 Heat 2 tablespoons of the orange juice with the saffron until almost boiling, then remove from the heat and let stand for 10 minutes.

3 Sift the flour and baking powder into a large bowl and add the butter, superfine sugar, and eggs. Beat well until the mixture is smooth, then stir in the orange rind and half of the saffron-and-orange juice mixture.

4 Divide the batter among the paper liners. Bake in the preheated oven for 12–15 minutes, or until risen, firm, and golden brown. Transfer the cupcakes to a wire rack and let cool.

5 Combine the remaining saffron-and-orange juice mixture and the confectioners' sugar to make a smooth paste, adding a little extra orange juice, if needed. Spoon a little on top of each cake, top with strips of orange zest, and let set.

tiramisu cupcakes

MAKES 12

½ **cup unsalted butter**

generous ½ **cup light brown sugar**

2 **eggs, beaten**

1 **cup self-rising flour, sifted**

½ **tsp baking powder**

2 **tsp instant coffee powder**

¼ **cup confectioners' sugar**

4 **tbsp water**

2 **tbsp finely grated semisweet chocolate, for dusting**

frosting

1 **cup mascarpone cheese**

scant ½ **cup superfine sugar**

2 **tbsp marsala or sweet sherry**

1 Preheat the oven to 350°F/180°C. Put 12 paper liners in a muffin pan or put 12 double-layer liners on a large baking sheet.

2 Put the butter, sugar, eggs, flour, and baking powder in a bowl and, using an electric mixer, beat together until smooth and creamy. Spoon the batter into the paper liners.

3 Bake the cupcakes for 15–20 minutes, until risen, golden, and firm to the touch.

4 Put the coffee powder, confectioners' sugar, and water in a small pan and heat gently, stirring until the coffee and sugar have dissolved. Boil for 1 minute, then let cool for 10 minutes. Use a pastry brush to liberally brush the coffee syrup over the top of the warm cakes. Transfer the cakes to a wire rack and let cool.

5 For the frosting, put the mascarpone, sugar, and marsala or sherry in a bowl and beat together until smooth. Spread over the top of the cakes. Using a stencil, decorate with the grated chocolate or simply sprinkle the grated chocolate over the frosting.

Step
2

Step
4

Step
5

banana & caramel cupcakes

5 tbsp butter, softened, plus extra for greasing

½ cup light brown sugar

2 eggs, lightly beaten

¾ cup self-rising flour

1 small ripe banana, peeled and mashed

topping

⅔ cup heavy cream

½ banana, peeled and sliced

2 tbsp dulce de leche

1 tbsp grated chocolate

1 Preheat the oven to 375°F/190°C. Grease four 1-cup ovenproof dishes (such as ramekins) with butter.

2 Put the butter and sugar in a bowl and beat together until light and fluffy. Gradually beat in the eggs. Sift in the flour and, using a metal spoon, fold into the mixture with the mashed banana. Spoon the batter into the dishes.

3 Put the dishes on a baking sheet and bake in the preheated oven for 20–25 minutes, or until risen and golden brown. Let cool.

4 For the topping, whisk the cream in a bowl until softly peaking. Spoon the whipped cream on top of each cupcake, then arrange 3–4 banana slices on top. Drizzle over the dulce de leche and sprinkle over the grated chocolate. Store the cupcakes in the refrigerator until ready to serve.

raspberry ripple cupcakes

1½ cups all-purpose flour

1 tbsp baking powder

1 tbsp cornstarch

¾ cup unsalted butter, softened

generous ¾ cup superfine sugar

3 eggs, beaten

1 tsp almond extract

generous 1 cup fresh raspberries

vanilla sugar, for sprinkling

1 Preheat the oven to 375°F/190°C. Put 32 paper liners into shallow muffin pans or put 32 double-layer liners onto baking sheets.

2 Sift the flour, baking powder, and cornstarch into a large bowl and add the butter, sugar, eggs, and almond extract. Beat well until the mixture is smooth. Mash the raspberries lightly with a fork, then fold into the mix.

3 Divide the batter among the paper liners. Bake in the preheated oven for 15–20 minutes, or until risen, firm, and golden brown. Transfer the cupcakes to a wire rack to cool. Sprinkle with the vanilla sugar before serving.

strawberry & cream cupcakes

MAKES 10

6 tbsp unsalted butter, softened

scant ½ cup superfine sugar

½ tsp vanilla extract

1 extra large egg, lightly beaten

scant ⅔ cup self-rising flour

1 tbsp milk

¼ cup raisins

⅔ cup small strawberry slices

1 tbsp strawberry jelly

½ cup heavy cream, softly whipped

confectioners' sugar, for dusting

1 Preheat the oven to 375°F/190°C. Put 10 paper liners in a muffin pan or put 10 double-layer paper liners on a baking sheet.

2 Put the butter, sugar, and vanilla extract in a mixing bowl and beat together until light and fluffy. Gradually beat in the egg. Sift in the flour and, using a metal spoon, fold into the mixture with the milk and raisins. Spoon the batter into the paper liners.

3 Bake the cupcakes in the preheated oven for 15–20 minutes, or until golden brown and firm to the touch. Transfer to a wire rack and let cool.

4 When the cupcakes are cold, use a serrated knife to cut a circle from the top of each cupcake. Gently mix the strawberries and jelly together and divide among the cupcakes. Top each with a small dollop of the whipped cream. Replace the cake tops and dust with confectioners' sugar. Store the cupcakes in the refrigerator until ready to serve.

feather-iced coffee cupcakes

MAKES 18

½ **cup butter, softened**

⅔ **cup light brown sugar**

2 eggs

generous ¾ cup self-rising flour

½ **tsp baking powder**

1 tbsp instant coffee powder dissolved in 1 tbsp boiling water and cooled

2 tbsp sour cream

icing

2 cups confectioners' sugar

4 tsp warm water

1 tbsp instant coffee powder dissolved in 2 tbsp boiling water

1 Preheat the oven to 375°F/190°C. Put 18 paper liners in 2 muffin pans or put 18 double-layer paper liners on 2 baking sheets.

2 Put the butter, sugar, and eggs in a bowl. Sift in the flour and baking powder, then beat together until smooth. Add the dissolved coffee and sour cream and beat together until well mixed. Spoon the batter into the paper liners. Bake the cupcakes in the preheated oven for 20 minutes, or until well risen and golden brown. Transfer to a wire rack and let cool.

3 To make the icing, sift 1¼ cup of the confectioners' sugar into a bowl, then gradually mix in the water. Sift the remaining confectioners' sugar into a separate bowl, then stir in the dissolved coffee. Put the coffee icing in a pastry bag, fitted with a narrow tip. When the cupcakes are cold, coat the tops with the white icing and pipe the coffee icing across in parallel lines. Draw a skewer across the piped lines in both directions.

Step 2

Step 2

Step 3

lemon meringue cupcakes

MAKES 4

6 tbsp butter, softened, plus extra for greasing

scant ½ cup superfine sugar

finely grated rind and juice of ½ lemon

1 extra large egg, lightly beaten

scant ⅔ cup self-raising flour

2 tbsp lemon curd

meringue

2 egg whites

generous ½ cup superfine sugar

1 Preheat the oven to 375°F/190°C. Grease four 1-cup ovenproof dishes (such as ramekins) with butter.

2 Put the butter, sugar, and lemon rind in a bowl and beat together until light and fluffy. Gradually beat in the egg. Sift in the flour and, using a metal spoon, fold into the mixture with the lemon juice. Spoon the batter into the dishes.

3 Put the dishes on a baking sheet and bake in the preheated oven for 15 minutes, or until risen and pale golden brown.

4 While the cupcakes are baking, make the meringue. Put the egg whites in a clean grease-free bowl and, using a electric mixer, mix until stiff. Gradually beat in the superfine sugar to form a stiff and glossy meringue.

5 Spread the lemon curd over the hot cupcakes, then swirl over the meringue. Return the cupcakes to the oven for 4–5 minutes, until the meringue is golden. Serve immediately.

caramel apple cupcakes

MAKES 18

2 apples

1 tbsp lemon juice

2¼ cups all-purpose flour

2 tsp baking powder

1½ tsp ground cinnamon

generous ¼ cup light brown sugar

4 tbsp butter, plus extra for greasing

scant ½ cup milk

scant ½ cup apple juice

1 egg, beaten

caramel topping

2 tbsp light cream

3 tbsp light brown sugar

1 tbsp butter

1 Preheat the oven to 400°F/200°C. Grease the cups in two 9-cup muffin pans, preferably nonstick.

2 Core and coarsely grate one of the apples. Slice the remaining apple into ¼-inch/5-mm-thick wedges and toss in the lemon juice. Sift together the flour, baking powder, and cinnamon, then stir in the sugar and grated apple.

3 Melt the butter and mix with the milk, apple juice, and egg. Stir the liquid mixture into the dry ingredients, mixing lightly until just combined. Spoon the batter into the prepared muffin pans. Put two apple slices on top of each cake.

4 Bake in the preheated oven for 20–25 minutes, or until risen, firm, and golden brown. Run a knife around the edge of each cake to loosen, then turn out onto a wire rack to cool.

5 For the topping, place all the ingredients in a small pan and heat, stirring, until the sugar has dissolved. Increase the heat and boil rapidly for 2 minutes, or until slightly thickened and syrupy. Cool slightly, then drizzle over the cakes and let set.

honey & spice cupcakes

MAKES 12

⅔ cup butter

scant ½ cup light brown sugar

scant ½ cup honey

1¾ cups self-rising flour

1 tsp ground allspice

2 eggs, beaten

12 whole blanched almonds

1 Preheat the oven to 350°F/180°C. Put 12 paper liners in a muffin pan or put 12 double-layer paper liners on a baking sheet.

2 Place the butter, sugar, and honey in a large pan and heat gently, stirring, until the butter has melted. Remove the pan from the heat.

3 Sift together the flour and allspice and stir into the mixture in the pan, then beat in the eggs, mixing to a smooth batter.

4 Spoon the batter into the paper liners and place a blanched almond on top of each one. Bake in the preheated oven for 20–25 minutes, or until well-risen and golden brown. Transfer to a wire rack and let cool.

24-carrot gold cupcakes

MAKES 12

¾ cup butter, softened, or soft margarine

generous ½ cup superfine sugar

2 eggs, lightly beaten

generous 1½ cup grated carrot

½ cup finely chopped walnuts

2 tbsp orange juice

grated rind of ½ orange

1½ cups self-rising flour

1 tsp ground cinnamon

12 walnut halves, for decorating

frosting

½ cup cream cheese

2 cups confectioners' sugar

1 tbsp orange juice

1 Preheat the oven to 350°F/180°C. Line a 12-cup muffin pan with 12 paper liners.

2 Place the butter and sugar in a large bowl and beat together until light and fluffy, then gradually beat in the eggs. Fold in the grated carrot, walnuts, and orange juice and rind. Sift in the flour and cinnamon and fold into the batter until just combined. Spoon the batter into the paper liners.

3 Bake in the preheated oven for 15–20 minutes, or until golden and springy to the touch. Transfer to a wire rack and let cool completely.

4 To make the frosting, place the cream cheese, confectioners' sugar, and orange juice in a bowl and beat together. Spread over the top of the cakes, then decorate with the walnut halves.

VARIATION

To make 9-carrot gold cupcakes, use ½ cup grated carrot and ¾ cup grated zuchinni, and replace the walnuts with ⅓ cup golden raisins. Decorate the top of each cake with pecans.

almonds
    almond & apricot spice cupcakes 144
    cherry & almond cupcakes 52
    chocolate fruit & nut cupcakes 102
    christmas cupcakes 168
    honey & spice cupcakes 204
    iced almond & lemon cupcakes 22
    lemon & raspberry cupcakes 110
    marzipan chunk cupcakes 56
    marzipan flower cupcakes 162
    pure indulgence almond cupcakes 152
    raspberry almond cupcakes 128
    shredded orange cupcakes 124
anniversary cupcakes 182
apples
    apple pie cupcakes 164
    apple streusel cupcakes 140
    caramel apple cupcakes 202
apricots
    almond & apricot spice cupcakes 144
    whole wheat apricot cupcakes 136

baby shower cupcakes 178
bananas
    banana & caramel cupcakes 192
    banana & pecan cupcakes 148
    hummingbird cupcakes 132
birthday party cupcakes 166
blackberry crumble cupcakes 130
blueberries
    buttermilk cupcakes 122
    iced blueberry cupcakes 120
buttermilk cupcakes 122
butterscotch cupcakes 30

candies
    birthday party cupcakes 166
    mini candy cupcakes 14
caramel cupcakes 28
carrots
    24-carrot gold cupcakes 206
    carrot & orange cupcakes 126
cherries
    cherry & almond cupcakes 52
    chocolate & cherry cupcakes 94
    cherry cupcakes 184
    chocolate fruit & nut cupcakes 102
    chocolate & cherry cupcakes 94
    coconut cherry cupcakes 142
    rocky road cupcakes 78
    sugar & spice cupcakes 44
chocolate
    banana & caramel cupcakes 192
    chocolate brownie cupcakes 70
    chocolate butterfly cupcakes 62
    chocolate & cherry cupcakes 94
    chocolate chip cupcakes 98
    chocolate curl cupcakes 74
    chocolate fruit & nut cupcakes 102
    chocolate & hazelnut cupcakes 86
    chocolate & orange cupcakes 92
    chocolate-topped cupcakes 60
    dark & white cupcakes 80
    devil's food cupcakes 72
    double chocolate cupcakes 68
    frosted chocolate cupcakes 66
    hot pecan brownie cupcakes 88
    marbled chocolate cupcakes 106
    mocha cupcakes 90
    molten-centered chocolate cupcakes 64
    pear & chocolate cupcakes 96
    peppermint cupcakes 84
    red velvet cupcakes 32
    rocky road cupcakes 78
    tiny chocolate cupcakes 104
    tiramisu cupcakes 190
    valentine heart cupcakes 172
    white chocolate & rose cupcakes 82
    white chocolate chip cupcakes 100
christmas cupcakes 168

coconut
    coconut cherry cupcakes 142
    pink & white cupcakes 18
coffee
    coffee fudge cupcakes 160
    feather-iced coffee cupcakes 198
    mocha cupcakes 90
    tiramisu cupcakes 190
    cranberry cupcakes 134
cream cheese
    24-carrot gold cupcakes 206
    carrot & orange cupcakes 126
    cherry cupcakes 184
    chocolate curl cupcakes 74
    frosted peanut butter cupcakes 48
    hummingbird cupcakes 132
    lemon cornmeal cupcakes 20
    macadamia & maple cupcakes 150
    pineapple tropical cupcakes 116
    red velvet cupcakes 32
    tiramisu cupcakes 190
    white chocolate & rose cupcakes 82

dates: sticky date cupcakes 154
devil's food cupcakes 72
dried fruit
    chocolate fruit & nut cupcakes 102
    earl grey cupcakes 42
    festive cupcakes 170
    fudge & raisin cupcakes 34
    queen cupcakes 40
    strawberry & cream cupcakes 196
dulce de leche
    almond & apricot spice cupcakes 144
    banana & caramel cupcakes 192

earl grey cupcakes 42
easter cupcakes 174

fairy cupcakes 12
festive cupcakes 170
fondant
    christmas cupcakes 168
    gold star cupcakes 180
    halloween cupcakes 176
fudge & raisin cupcakes 34

gingerbread cupcakes 54
gold star cupcakes 180

halloween cupcakes 176
hazelnuts
    chocolate & nut cupcakes 86
    spiced plum cupcakes 138
    vanilla hazelnut yogurt cupcakes 186
honey
    chocolate & sponge toffee cupcakes 76
    drizzled honey cupcakes 36
    honey & spice cupcakes 204
    mocha cupcakes 90
    pear & chocolate cupcakes 96
hummingbird cupcakes 132

jelly cupcakes 46

lemons
    baby shower cupcakes 178
    iced almond & lemon cupcakes 22
    lemon butterfly cupcakes 112
    lemon crunch cupcakes 114
    lemon meringue cupcakes 200
    lemon cornmeal cupcakes 20
    lemon & raspberry cupcakes 110

macadamia & maple cupcakes 150
mango & passion fruit cupcakes 118
maple syrup
    hot pecan brownie cupcakes 88
    macadamia & maple cupcakes 150
marshmallows: rocky road cupcakes 78

marzipan
    marzipan chunk cupcakes 56
    marzipan flower cupcakes 162
    valentine heart cupcakes 172
mocha cupcakes 90

nuts
    frosted peanut butter cupcakes 48
    macadamia & maple cupcakes 150
    pistachio cupcakes 146
    rocky road cupcakes 78
    see also almonds; hazelnuts;
    pecans; walnuts
oats: chewy oatmeal-topped
    cupcakes 50
oranges
    24-carrot gold cupcakes 206
    carrot & orange cupcakes 126
    chocolate & orange cupcakes 92
    drizzled honey cupcakes 36
    festive cupcakes 170
    hot marmalade cupcakes 38
    mango & passion fruit cupcakes 118
    orange saffron mini cupcakes 188
    poppy seed & orange cupcakes 24
    shredded orange cupcakes 124

passion fruit: mango & passion
fruit cupcakes 118
pear & chocolate cupcakes 96
pecan nuts
    banana & pecan cupcakes 148
    hot pecan brownie cupcakes 88
    hummingbird cupcakes 132
peppermint cupcakes 84
pineapple
    hummingbird cupcakes 132
    pineapple tropical cupcakes 116
pistachio cupcakes 146
plums: spiced plum cupcakes 138
poppy seed & orange cupcakes 24

queen cupcakes 40

raspberries
    lemon & raspberry cupcakes 110
    raspberry almond cupcakes 128
    raspberry ripple cupcakes 194
red velvet cupcakes 32
rocky road cupcakes 78
rose petal cupcakes 16

sour cream
    banana & pecan cupcakes 148
    devil's food cupcakes 72
    feather-iced coffee cupcakes 198
    iced blueberry cupcakes 120
strawberries
    strawberry & cream cupcakes 196
    warm strawberry cupcakes 26

tiramisu cupcakes 190

valentine heart cupcakes 172
vanilla frosted cupcakes 10
vanilla hazelnut yogurt
    cupcakes 186

walnuts
    24-carrot gold cupcakes 206
    carrot & orange cupcakes 126
    chocolate brownie cupcakes 70
    drizzed honey cupcakes 36
    moist walnut cupcakes 156
    whole wheat apricot cupcakes 136